The St. Martin's Pocket Guide to Research and Documentation

Fourth Edition

ADAPTED FROM

The St. Martin's Handbook
Sixth Edition

ANDREA A. LUNSFORD
MARCIA MUTH

BEDFORD / ST. MARTIN'S
Boston ♦ New York

Manufactured in the United States of America.

1 0 9 8 7
f   e   d   c   b   a

For information, write: Bedford/St. Martin's, 75 Arlington Street, Boston, MA 02116   (617-399-4000)

ISBN-10: 0-312-44225-4
ISBN-13: 978-0-312-44225-5

Acknowledgments

Page 215: Rebecca M. Chory-Assad and Ron Tamborini. Excerpt from "Television Sitcom Exposure and Aggressive Communication: A Priming Perspective." From the *North American Journal of Psychology* 15630823: 2004, Vol. 6, Issue 3. Reprinted with permission of the publisher; **pages 23–24, 215:** *EBSCO* Information Services. Screenshots of EBSCO Host Research Database; **page 255:** Alan L. Miller. Excerpt from "Epidemiology, etiology, and natural treatment of seasonal affective disorder." From *Alternative Medicine Review,* March 2005; 10 (1): 5–13. Reprinted with permission.

Contents

8   Research in the Applied Sciences   266

Introduction

The St. Martin's Pocket Guide to Research and Documentation, Fourth Edition, is small enough to fit in your pocket but big enough to provide all the speedy and reliable help you'll need with research assignments from across the disciplines, including advice for planning, conducting, and documenting your research. Specifically, this guide provides

- general advice on the research process:
    - narrowing and focusing a topic
    - finding and evaluating sources in the library and on the Web
    - taking notes
    - acknowledging sources and avoiding plagiarism
- general resource materials useful in many fields
- specialized resources useful in particular disciplines
- documentation guidelines for five styles:
    - MLA (Modern Language Association)
    - *Chicago* (*Chicago Manual of Style*)
    - APA (American Psychological Association)
    - CSE (Council of Science Editors)
    - AIP (American Institute of Physics)

- sample student research assignments that show how to incorporate research materials and document sources
- innovative new source maps that annotate sample sources, giving step-by-step guidelines to help you evaluate and cite print and electronic materials
- integrated library research coverage to help you navigate today's wired libraries
- guidelines for avoiding plagiarism and knowing how to quote, paraphrase, and summarize sources

In the lists of resource materials, print materials that are also available online are noted accordingly. Online versions of most research resources require paid subscriptions; therefore you will probably want to access them through a library computer. If a Web address (URL) is given, the online version does not require a subscription.

1

Preparing for a Research Project

Narrowing a Topic

Any topic you choose to research must be manageable — it must suit the scope, audience, length, and time limits of your assignment. Making a topic manageable often requires narrowing it, but you may also need to find a particular slant and look for a question to guide your research. To arrive at such a question, you might first generate a series of questions about your topic. You can then evaluate them and choose one or two that are both interesting and manageable. The result of the narrowing process is a research question that can be tentatively answered by a hypothesis, a statement of what you anticipate your research will show.

Like a working thesis, a hypothesis must be manageable, interesting, and specific. In addition, it must be arguable, a debatable proposition that you can prove or disprove with a reasonable amount of research evidence. For example, a statement like this one is not arguable since it merely states a widely known fact: "Senator Joseph McCarthy attracted great attention with his anti-Communist crusade during the 1950s." On the other hand, this statement is an arguable hypothesis because evidence for or against it can be found: "Roy Cohn's biased research while he was an assistant to Senator Joseph

McCarthy was partially responsible for McCarthy's anti-Communist crusade."

In moving from a general topic of interest, such as Senator Joseph McCarthy's anti-Communist crusade of the 1950s, to a useful hypothesis, such as the one in the previous paragraph, you first narrow the topic to a single manageable issue: Roy Cohn's role in the crusade, for instance. After background reading, you then raise a question about that issue ("To what extent did Cohn's research contribute to McCarthy's crusade?") and devise a possible answer, your hypothesis. The hypothesis, which tentatively answers your research question, must be precise enough to be supported or challenged by a manageable amount of research.

As you gather information and begin reading and evaluating sources, you will probably refine your research question and change your hypothesis significantly. Only after you have explored your hypothesis, tested it, and sharpened it by reading, writing, and talking with others does it become a working thesis.

In doing your own research, you may find that your interest shifts, that a whole line of inquiry is unproductive, or that your hypothesis is simply wrong. In each case, the process of research pushes you to learn more about your hypothesis, to make it more precise, to become an expert on your topic.

Determining What You Know

Once you have formulated a hypothesis, determine what you already know about your topic. Here are some strategies for doing so:

- *Brainstorming.* Take five minutes to list everything you think of or wonder about your hypothesis. You may find it helpful to do this in a group with other students.

- *Freewriting about your hypothesis.* For five minutes, write about every reason for believing your hypothesis is true. Then for another five minutes, write down every argument you can think of, no matter how weak, that someone opposed to your hypothesis might make.

- *Freewriting about your audience.* Write for five minutes about your readers, including your instructor. What do you think they currently believe about your topic? What sorts of evidence will convince them to accept your hypothesis? What sorts of sources will they respect?
- *Tapping your memory for sources.* List everything you can remember about where you learned about your topic: Web sites, email, books, magazines, courses, conversations, television. What you know comes from somewhere, and that "somewhere" can serve as a starting point for research.

Preliminary Research Plan

Once you've considered what you already know about your topic, you can develop a research plan. To do so, answer the following questions:

- What kinds of sources (books, journal articles, databases, Web sites, government documents, specialized reference works, images, videos, and so on) will you need to consult? How many sources should you consult?
- How current do your sources need to be? (For topical issues, especially those related to science, current sources are usually most important. For historical subjects, older sources may offer the best information.)
- How can you determine the location and availability of the kinds of sources you need?
- Do you need to consult sources contemporary with an event or a person's life? If so, how will you get access to those sources?

One goal of your research plan is to begin building a strong working bibliography (Chapter 3). Carrying out systematic research and keeping careful notes on your sources will make developing your works-cited list or bibliography (Chapters 5–8) easier later on.

2

Conducting Research

Kinds of Sources

Sources can include data from interviews and surveys, books and articles in print and online, Web sites, film, video, images, and more. Consider these important differences among sources.

Primary and Secondary Sources

Primary sources provide firsthand knowledge, while secondary sources report on or analyze the research of others. Primary sources are basic sources of raw information, including your own field research; films, works of art, or other objects you examine; literary works you read; and eyewitness accounts, photographs, news reports, and historical documents (such as letters and speeches). Secondary sources are descriptions or interpretations of primary sources, such as researchers' reports, reviews, biographies, and encyclopedia articles. Often what constitutes a primary or secondary source depends on the purpose of your research. A critic's evaluation of a film, for instance, serves as a secondary source if you are writing about the film but as a primary source if you are studying the critic's writing.

Most research projects draw on both primary and secondary sources. A research-based essay on the effects of steroid use on major league baseball, for example, might draw on primary sources, such as the players' testimony to Congress, as well as secondary sources, such as articles or books by baseball experts.

Scholarly and Popular Sources

While nonacademic sources like magazines and personal Web sites can help you get started on a research project, you will usually want to depend more heavily on authorities in a field, whose work generally appears in scholarly journals in print or online. The following list will help you distinguish scholarly and popular sources:

SCHOLARLY

- Title often contains the word *Journal*
- Source available mainly through libraries and library databases
- Few commercial advertisements
- Authors identified with academic credentials
- Summary or abstract appears on first page of article; articles are fairly long
- Articles cite sources and provide bibliographies

POPULAR

- *Journal* usually does not appear in title
- Source generally available outside of libraries (at newsstands or from a home Internet connection)
- Many advertisements
- Authors are usually journalists or reporters hired by the publication, not academics or experts
- No summary or abstract; articles are fairly short
- Articles may include quotations but do not cite sources or provide bibliographies

Older and More Current Sources

Most projects can benefit from both older, historical sources and more current ones. Some older sources are classics in their fields, essential for understanding the scholarship that follows them. Others are simply dated, though even these works can be useful to researchers who want to see what people wrote and read about a topic in the past. Depending on your purpose, you may rely primarily on recent sources (for example, if you are writing about a new scientific discovery), primarily on historical sources (if your project discusses a nineteenth-century industrial accident), or on a mixture of both. Whether a source appeared hundreds of years ago or this morning, evaluate it carefully to determine how useful it will be for you.

Using the Library to Get Started

Even when you have a general idea of what kinds of sources exist and which kinds you need for your research project, you still have to locate these sources. Many beginning researchers are tempted to assume that all the information they could possibly need is readily available on the Internet from a home connection. However, it is a good idea to begin almost any research project with the sources available in your college library.

Reference Librarians

You might start by getting to know one particularly valuable resource, your library staff—especially reference librarians. You can make an appointment to talk with a librarian about your research project and get specific recommendations about databases and other helpful places to begin your research. In addition, many libraries have online chat environments where students can ask questions about their research and have them answered, in real time, by a reference librarian. To get the most helpful advice, whether online or in person, pose *specific* questions—not "Where can I find information about computers?" but "Where can I find information on the history of instant-message technologies?" If you are having difficulty asking precise questions, you probably need to do some background research on your topic and formulate a sharper hypothesis. A librarian may be helpful in this regard as well.

Catalogs and Databases

Your library's computers hold many resources not available on the Web or not accessible to students except through the library's system. One of these resources is the library's own catalog of books and other holdings, but most college libraries also subscribe to a large number of databases — electronic collections of information, such as indexes to journal and magazine articles, texts of news stories and legal cases, lists of sources on particular topics, and compilations of statistics — that students can access for free. Many of these databases — such as LexisNexis, MLA Bibiliography, and ERIC — have been screened or compiled by editors, librarians, or other scholars. Your library may also have metasearch software that allows you to search several databases at once.

Reference Works

Consulting general reference works is another good way to get started on a research project. These works are especially helpful for getting an overview of a topic, identifying subtopics, finding more specialized sources, and identifying useful keywords for electronic searches.

The following guides to reference works can help you identify those that suit your purpose:

Gale Directory of Databases. 2 vols. 1993–; annual. This two-volume resource is the most comprehensive index and guide to databases available. (online)

Guide to Reference Books. Edited by Robert Balay. 11th ed. 1996. This large book supplies annotated lists of general reference works and specialized bibliographies and is divided into five sections: General Reference; Humanities; Social and Behavioral Sciences; History and Area Studies; and Science, Technology, and Medicine. Each section is further subdivided into areas and then into special approaches. Full bibliographic information, including Library of Congress call number, is provided for each entry.

The New Walford: Guide to Reference Resources. 8th ed. 3 vols. 2005–2008. *The New Walford*'s three volumes deal with Science, Technology, and Medicine; the Social Sciences; and Arts, Humanities, and General Reference.

GENERAL ENCYCLOPEDIAS

For general background on a subject, encyclopedias are a good place to begin, particularly because many include bibliographies that can point you to more specialized sources. A librarian can direct you to such reference works. Remember that encyclopedias will serve as a place to start your research — not as major sources for a research project.

SPECIALIZED ENCYCLOPEDIAS

Compared with general encyclopedias, specialized encyclopedias — on subjects from ancient history to world drama — usually provide more detailed articles by authorities in the field as well as extensive bibliographies for locating sources. Again, you should rely on these works more for background material than as major sources of information. Many specialized encyclopedias are available online as well as in print. For more information on specialized encyclopedias in particular fields, see Chapters 5–8.

BIOGRAPHICAL RESOURCES

The lives and historical settings of famous people are the topics of biographical dictionaries and indexes. Here are a few examples of biographical reference works; many others, particularly volumes specialized by geographic area or field, are available.

African American Biographies: Profiles of 558 Current Men and Women. 1992. Profiles over five hundred notable African Americans.

American Men and Women of Science. 27th ed. 2007. Formerly *American Men of Science.* Provides biographical information on notable scientists alive today. (online)

Biography Index. 1946–; quarterly. Lists biographical material found in current books and over twenty-six hundred periodicals. (online)

Contemporary Authors. 1962–; annual. Supplies short biographies of authors who have published works during the year. (online)

Current Biography. 1940–; monthly, with annual cumulations. Provides informative articles on people in the news. Includes photographs and short biographies. (online)

Dictionary of American Biography. 1927–1936; supplements 1944–1980. Contains biographies of over fifteen thousand deceased Americans from all phases of public life from colonial days to 1980. Entries include bibliographies of sources. (online)

International Who's Who. 1935–; annual. Contains biographies of persons of international status.

Merriam Webster's Biographical Dictionary. 1995. Provides biographical information on important deceased people of the last five thousand years.

Notable American Women: 1607–1950. 3 vols. 1972. Supplement, *Notable American Women: The Modern Period.* 1980. Supplement, *Notable American Women: A Biographical Dictionary Completing the Twentieth Century.* 2004. Contains biographies (with bibliographies) of women who contributed to North American society. The supplement covers women who died between 1951 and 1975.

Oxford Dictionary of National Biography. 2004. Covers deceased notables from Great Britain and its colonies (excluding the post-colonial United States).

Who's Who. 1849–; annual. Covers well-known living British people. *Who Was Who,* with volumes covering about a decade each, lists British notables who died between 1897 and the present.

Who's Who in America. 1899–; annual. Covers famous living North Americans. Notable Americans no longer living are in *Who Was Who in America,* covering 1607 to the present. Similar specialized works include *Who's Who of American Women, Who's Who in the World, Who's Who in Asia,* and so on. (online)

ALMANACS, YEARBOOKS, AND NEWS DIGESTS

Almanacs, yearbooks, and news digests provide information on current events and statistical data.

Facts on File: News Digest. 1941–; weekly. Summarizes and indexes facts about current events. (online)

Information Please Almanac. 1947–; annual. Includes many charts, facts, and lists as well as short summaries of the year's events and accomplishments in various fields. (online at www.infoplease.com/almanacs.html)

The Statesman's Yearbook. 1863–; annual. Contains current facts and statistics about the agriculture, government, population, development, religion, and so on of the countries of the world. (online)

Statistical Abstract of the United States. 1878–; annual. Published by the Bureau of the Census; provides government data on U.S. population, business, immigration, and other subjects. (online at www.census.gov/compendia/statab)

World Almanac and Book of Facts. 1868–; annual. Presents data and statistics on business, education, sports, government, population, and other topics. Includes institutional names and addresses and reviews important annual public events. (online)

ATLASES

In addition to physical maps of all parts of the world, the following atlases contain maps showing population, food distribution, mineral concentrations, temperature and rainfall, and political borders, among other facts and statistics.

Atlas of World Cultures: A Geographical Guide to Ethnographic Literature. 2004.
Hammond World Atlas. 2003.
National Geographic Atlas of the World. 2005.
The Rand McNally Commercial Atlas and Marketing Guide. 2006.
The Times Comprehensive Atlas of the World. 2005.

Finding Library Resources

The library is one of a researcher's best friends, especially in an age of electronic communication. Your college library houses a great number of print materials and gives you access to electronic catalogs, indexes, and databases. But the library may seem daunting to you, especially on your first visit. Experienced student researchers will tell you that the best way to make the library a friend is to get to know it: a good starting place is its Web site, where you can find useful information, including its hours of operation, its floor plan, its collections, and so on; many libraries also have a virtual tour and other tutorials on their Web sites that give you a first-rate introduction to getting the most out of the library's resources.

Searching Catalogs and Databases

The most important tools your library offers are its online catalog and databases. Searching these tools will always be easier and more efficient if you use carefully chosen words to limit the scope of your research.

SUBJECT WORD SEARCHING

Catalogs and databases usually index their contents not only by author and title, but also by subject headings — standardized words

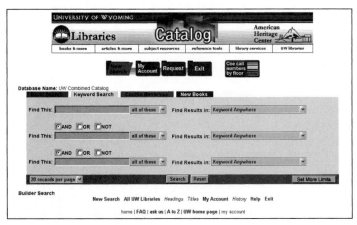

Advanced search page from a library catalog that incorporates Boolean operators

and phrases used to classify the subject matter of books and articles. (For books, most U.S. academic libraries use the *Library of Congress Subject Headings,* or LCSH, for this purpose.) When you search the catalog by subject, you need to use the exact subject words.

KEYWORD SEARCHING

Searches using keywords, on the other hand, make use of the computer's ability to look for any term in any field of the electronic record, including not just subject but also author, title, series, and notes. In article databases, a keyword search will look in abstracts and summaries of articles as well. Keyword searching is less restrictive, but it requires you to put some thought into choosing your search terms in order to get the best results.

ADVANCED SEARCHING

Many library catalogs and database search engines offer advanced search options (sometimes on a separate page) to help you combine keywords, search for an exact phrase, or exclude items containing particular keywords. Often they let you limit your search in other ways as well, such as by date, language, country of origin, or location of the keyword within a site.

Many catalogs and databases offer a search option using the Boolean operators AND, OR, and NOT, and some allow you to use parentheses to refine your search or wildcards to expand it. Note that much Boolean decision making is done for you when you use an advanced search option (as on the advanced search page shown on the opposite page). Note, too, that search engines vary in the exact terms and symbols they use to refine searches, so check before you search.

- AND *limits your search.* If you enter the terms *IM* AND *language* AND *literacy,* the search engine will retrieve only those items that contain all the terms. Some search engines use a plus sign (+) instead of AND.

- OR *expands your search.* If you enter the terms *IM* OR *language,* the computer will retrieve every item that contains the term *IM* and every item that contains the term *language.*

- NOT *limits your search.* If you enter the terms *IM* NOT *language,* the search engine will retrieve every item that contains *IM* except those that also contain the term *language.* Some search engines use a minus sign (–) or AND NOT instead of NOT.

- *Parentheses customize your search.* Entering *IM* AND (*literacy* OR *linguistics*), for example, will locate items that mention either of those terms in connection with instant messaging.

- *Wildcards expand your search.* Use a wildcard, usually an asterisk (*) or a question mark (?), to find related words that begin with the same letters. Entering *messag** will locate *message, messages,* and *messaging.*

- *Quotation marks narrow your search.* Most search engines interpret words within quotation marks as a phrase that must appear with the words in that exact order.

Books

CATALOG INFORMATION

The library catalog lists all the library's books. Library catalogs follow a standard pattern of organization, with each holding identified by three kinds of entries: one headed by the *author's name,* one by the *title,* and one or (usually) more by the *subject.* If you can't find a particular source under any of these headings, you can search the catalog by using a combination of subject headings and keywords. Such searches may turn up other useful titles as well.

Following are a search page, a page of results for noted linguist and author David Crystal, and a catalog entry for one of his books from a university library catalog. Note that many electronic catalogs indicate whether a book has been checked out and, if so, when it is due to be returned. Sometimes, as in this case, you must click on a link to check the availability of the book.

Catalog entries for books list not only the author, title, subject, and publication information but also a call number that indicates how the book is classified and where it is shelved. Like many online catalogs, the catalog in the preceding examples allows you to save the information about the book while you continue searching and then

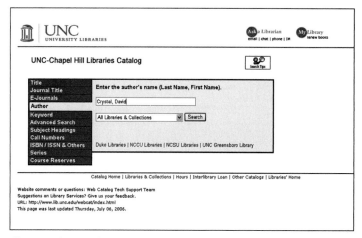

Library catalog search page

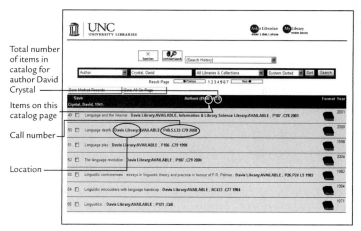

Results for author search in library catalog database

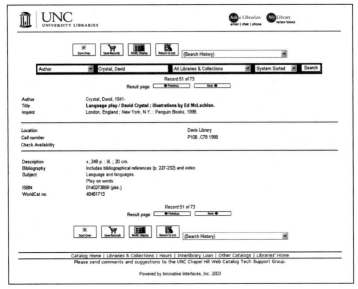

Catalog entry for a book chosen from author search

retrieve the call numbers for all of the books you want to find in one list. Once you have the call number for a book, look for a library map or shelving plan to tell you where the book is housed. Take the time to browse through the books near the call number you are looking for. Often you will find other books related to your topic in the immediate area.

INDEXES TO BOOKS AND REVIEWS

Book indexes can be helpful for quickly locating complete information on a book when you know only one piece of it — the author's last name, perhaps, or the title. These sources can also alert you to other works by a particular author or on a particular subject. Although book indexes are generally available online, you may need to consult the print version of an index for books and reviews written prior to 1996.

Books in Print. 1948–; annual. Lists by author, subject, and title all books distributed in the United States that are currently in print. (online)

Cumulative Book Index. 1898–; monthly. Lists by author, subject, and title books in English distributed in the United States and internationally. (online)

Paperbound Books in Print. 1955–; semiannual. Lists by author, subject, and title all paperback books distributed in the United States that are currently in print. (online)

Consider also using a review index to check the relevance of a source or to get a thumbnail sketch of its contents. Be sure to check not only the year of a book's publication but also the next year.

Annual Bibliography of English Language and Literature (ABELL). 1923–; annual. Lists monographs, periodical articles, critical editions, book reviews, and essay collections related to literary works. (online)

Book Review Digest. 1905–; annual. Contains excerpts from reviews of books along with information for locating the full reviews in popular and scholarly periodicals. (online)

Book Review Index. 1965–; annual. Identifies dates and locations for finding full reviews in several hundred popular and scholarly periodicals; organizes entries by the name of the book's author.

International Bibliography of Book Reviews (IBR). 1985–; monthly. Lists book reviews published in scholarly journals, primarily in the social sciences and humanities. (online)

Look also for specialized review indexes such as *Index to Book Reviews in the Humanities* and *Index to Book Reviews in the Social Sciences.*

Periodical Articles

Titles of periodicals held by a library appear in its catalog, but the titles of individual articles do not. To find the contents of periodicals, you will need to use an index source.

PERIODICAL INDEXES

Periodical indexes are databases or print volumes that hold information about articles published in newspapers, magazines, and scholarly journals. Different indexes cover different groups of periodicals; articles written before 1990 may be indexed only in a print volume. Ask a reference librarian for guidance about the most likely index for the subject of your research.

Electronic periodical indexes come in different forms, with some offering the full text of articles and some offering abstracts (short summaries) of the articles. Be sure not to confuse an abstract with a complete article. Full-text databases can be extremely convenient — you can read and print out articles directly from the computer, without the extra step of tracking down the periodical in question. However, don't limit yourself to full-text databases, which may not contain graphics and images that appeared in the print version of the periodical — and which may not include the sources that would benefit your research most. Take advantage of databases that offer abstracts, which give you an overview of the article's contents that can help you decide whether you need to spend time finding and reading the full text.

GENERAL INDEXES

General indexes of periodicals list articles from general-interest magazines (such as *Time* or *Newsweek*), newspapers, or a combination of these. Many major newspapers, such as the *New York Times,* and other periodicals have online archives, and some of their content can be accessed for free. General indexes usually provide current sources on a topic, but you may need to look further for in-depth articles. Online access to general indexes is usually available through your library. Ask a reference librarian for details.

Access: The Supplementary Index. 1979–; monthly. Indexes magazines not covered by the *Readers' Guide to Periodical Literature* (see below), such as regional and particular-interest magazines (the environment, women's issues). (online)

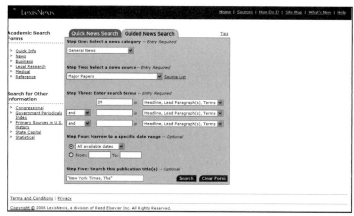

General index search for articles in the *New York Times*

Alternative Press Index. 1970–; monthly. Indexes alternative and radical publications.

InfoTrac. Updated monthly. Includes three indexes: (1) *General Periodicals Index* (current year and past four years), which covers over eleven

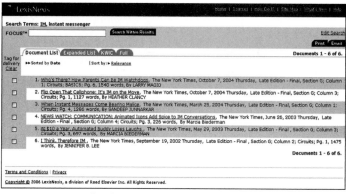

SEARCH WITHIN RESULTS hits from general index search

hundred general-interest publications, incorporating the *Magazine Index* and including the *New York Times* and *Wall Street Journal*; (2) *Academic Index* (current year and past four years), which covers over nine hundred scholarly and general-interest publications, including the *New York Times*; and (3) *National Newspaper Index* (current year and past three years). Some entries include a summary or even the entire article. (online)

LexisNexis Academic. 1974–. Lexis contains legal, legislative, and regulatory information. Nexis contains full texts and abstracts of newspapers, magazines, wire services, newsletters, company and industry analyst reports, and broadcast transcripts. (online)

Magazine Index. Updated monthly. Analyzes over five hundred general-interest magazines. (online)

National Newspaper Index. Updated monthly. Covers the *New York Times, Los Angeles Times, Wall Street Journal, Washington Post,* and *Christian Science Monitor.* (online)

NewsBank. 1970–; updated monthly. Includes articles from more than 2,000 newspapers.

New York Times Index. 1851–; bimonthly with annual cumulations. Lists by subject every article that has appeared in the *New York Times.* For most articles of any length, short summaries are given as well. (online)

Nineteenth Century Readers' Guide to Periodical Literature. 1890–1899. (See also *Readers' Guide,* below.)

Periodical Abstracts PlusText. 1986–. Contains abstracts of articles in over one thousand periodicals and journals in science, social science, humanities, and business. (online)

Poole's Index to Periodical Literature. 1802–1907. Indexes nineteenth-century British and American periodicals.

ProQuest Historical Newspapers. Ongoing project. Offers full-text digitized articles with images from nine major U.S. newspapers dating back to the 1700s. (online)

Readers' Guide to Periodical Literature. 1900–; semimonthly with quarterly and annual cumulations. Indexes articles from nearly four hundred magazines. Particularly helpful for social trends, popular scientific questions, and contemporary political issues. Entries are arranged by author and subject with cross-references to related topics. (online)

Times Index (London). 1913–; bimonthly. Lists articles and summaries of stories published in the London *Times*.

SPECIALIZED INDEXES AND ABSTRACTS

Many disciplines have specialized indexes and abstracts to help researchers find detailed information. In general, such works list articles in scholarly journals for that discipline, but they may include other publications as well. To use these resources most efficiently, ask a reference librarian to help you. For more information on specialized indexes and abstracts in particular fields, see Chapters 5–8. To use these resources most efficiently, ask a reference librarian to help you identify those most likely to address your topic. The two accompanying figures show examples of the results from a search of the specialized electronic index ERIC and of an article page with an abstract from ERIC.

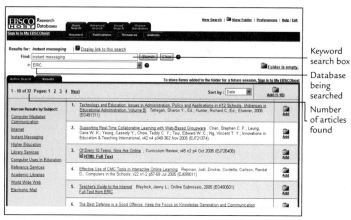

Results of search in a specialized index

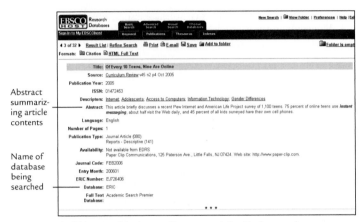

Abstract summarizing article contents

Name of database being searched

Article page with abstract from a specialized index search

LOCATING INDEXED PERIODICAL ARTICLES

To locate an indexed article that seems promising for your research project, you can check the library catalog to see whether the periodical is available electronically and, if so, whether your library has access to it. Using the library computer network for access can help you avoid paying to view the text of the article that is available online only for subscribers or for a fee.

If the periodical is not available electronically (some scholarly journals, for example, are not), the library catalog also will tell you whether a print version is available in your library's periodicals room. This room probably has recent issues of hundreds or even thousands of newspapers, magazines, and scholarly journals, and it may also contain bound volumes of past issues and microfilm copies of older newspapers.

Bibliographies

Look at any bibliographies (lists of sources) in books or articles you are using for your research; they can lead you to other valuable resources. In addition, check with a reference librarian to find out whether your library has more extensive bibliographies devoted to the area of your research.

Other Library Resources

In addition to books and periodicals, libraries give you access to many other useful materials that might be appropriate for your research.

- *Special collections and archives.* Your library may house archives (collections of valuable papers) and other special materials that are often available to student researchers. Ask a reference librarian whether they contain possible sources on your topic.
- *Audio, video, multimedia, and art collections.* Many libraries have areas devoted to media and art, where they collect films, videos, paintings, and sound recordings. Some libraries also let students check out laptops and other equipment for classroom presentations.
- *Government documents.* Many libraries have collections of historical documents produced by local or state government offices. Check with a librarian if government publications would be useful sources for your topic. You can also look at the online version of the U.S. Government Printing Office, known as GPO Access, for electronic versions of government publications from the past decade or so.
- *Interlibrary loans.* To borrow books, videos, or audio materials from another library, use an interlibrary loan. You can also request copies of journal articles from other libraries. Some loans — especially of books — can take time, so be sure to plan ahead.

Internet Research

The Internet is many college students' favorite way of accessing information, and it's true that much information — including authoritative sources identical to those your library provides — can be found online, sometimes for free. However, information in library databases comes from identifiable and professionally edited sources; because no one is responsible for regulating information on the Web, you need to take special care to find out which information online is reliable and which is not. (See Chapter 3 for more on evaluating sources.)

Internet Searches

The Internet offers two ways for you to search for sources: one using subject categories and one using keywords. Most Internet search tools, such as Yahoo! and Google, offer both options. A subject directory allows you to choose a broad category like "Science" and then to click on increasingly narrow categories like "Astronomy" or "The Solar System" until you reach a point where you are given a list of Web sites or the opportunity to do a keyword search. The second option, a search engine, allows you to start right off with a keyword search. Because the Internet contains vastly more material than even the largest library catalog or database, using a search engine requires even more care in the choice and combining of keywords. In an Internet search engine, you will need to choose keywords carefully in order to

GOOGLE'S SUBJECT DIRECTORY

get a reasonable number of hits. For example, if you enter *instant* and *messenger* and *language* as keywords in a Google search, you will get over seven million possible sources — a number too huge to be helpful for a researcher. To be useful, then, the keywords you choose — names, titles, authors, concepts — need to lead you to more specific sources. To follow the same example, a Google search for *"instant messenger language"* in quotation marks yields a much more manageable fifty results. Look for a search engine's search tips or advanced search options for help with refining and limiting a keyword search.

Although Yahoo! and Google are probably the most popular online search engines, the following list covers a broad range of search tools and their unique features.

AlltheWeb
www.alltheweb.com
   Allows keyword searches and has sophisticated advanced search options.

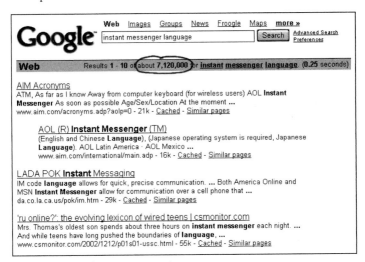

Google search yielding too many results

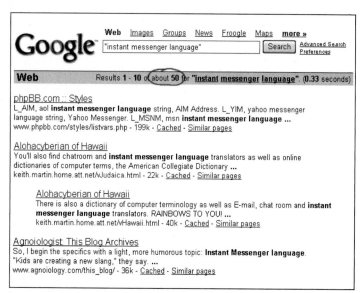

Google search using the same keywords in quotation marks

AltaVista

www.altavista.com

> Lets you search the entire Web using either a single keyword or multiple keywords.

Ask

www.ask.com

> Ranks results based on the number of same-subject pages that refer to it, not just general popularity.

Excite

www.excite.com

> Allows keyword and subject directory searches.

Google

www.google.com

> A popular search tool and a favorite among students; offers keyword and subject directory searches.

HotBot
www.hotbot.com
>Allows you to search one of several search engines and to narrow a search by specific dates, media, and other criteria. Offers keyword and subject directory searches.

Ixquick
www.ixquick.com
>A speedy metasearch tool that searches fourteen other engines or directories simultaneously using keywords.

Lycos
www.lycos.com
>Lets you search a huge catalog of Web sites as well as multimedia documents. Offers keyword and subject directory searches.

WebCrawler
www.webcrawler.com
>Searches several engines (including some that return sponsored listings) and subject directories.

Yahoo!
www.yahoo.com
>Allows you either to search directories of sites related to particular subjects (such as entertainment or education) or to enter keywords that Yahoo! gives to a search engine, which sends back the results.

Zworks
www.zworks.com
>Calls itself "the metasearch loved by parents and webmasters alike" because it can be filtered. Ranks results for relevancy.

Authoritative Sources Online

You can find many sources online that are authoritative and reliable. For example, the Internet enables you to enter virtual libraries that allow access to some collections in libraries other than your own. Online collections housed in government sites can also be reliable and useful sources.

Bureau of Labor Statistics
www.bls.gov
>Provides information by region and allows keyword searches.

The Library of Congress
www.loc.gov
> Offers a vast array of information on government legislation and copyright and intellectual property; a library catalog; and collections such as American Memory, which contains more than seven million digital items from over a hundred historical collections. Allows searches by title, author/creator, subject, and keyword.

National Institutes of Health
www.nih.gov
> Provides data on health and medical issues; allows keyword searches.

Statistical Abstract of the United States
www.census.gov/compendia/statab
> Provides information on social and economic trends; allows searches by keyword or place.

U.S. Census Bureau
www.census.gov
> Provides population and other demographic data; allows searches by keyword, place, and region.

For current national news, consult online versions of reputable newspapers such as the *New York Times,* the *Washington Post,* the *Los Angeles Times,* or the *Chicago Tribune* or electronic sites for news services such as CNN and C-SPAN. You can also use a search tool like Yahoo!, which has a "News and Media" category you can click on from the main page.

Some scholarly journals (such as those from Berkeley Electronic Press) and general-interest magazines (including *Slate* and *Salon*) are published only on the Web, and many other publications, like *Newsweek,* the *New Yorker,* and the *New Republic,* make at least some of their contents available online for free.

Discussion Lists

Many other people — friends, classmates, experts, and subscribers to electronic discussion lists — can lead you to sources or serve as sources themselves. For example, if you identify an expert you would like to interview, email that person and ask if she or he would agree to a brief online (or telephone) interview. You might also consider participating in a discussion list that is related to your topic. For example, Google Groups offers discussion groups on a wide variety of general interest topics, and you may also search its archive of Usenet newsgroups, which offers a twenty-year collection of over a billion messages. Your college library probably also subscribes to a number of electronic discussion lists. Remember, though, that not everyone involved in an online discussion will be an expert. As with any kind of research, choose online sources with care.

Internet Resources

The following general Web sites provide access to a wide range of information and more specialized sites.

American Library Association: Links to Library Web Resources
www.ala.org/library/weblinks.html
> Supplies links to notable library-related organizations and resources.

Infomine: Scholarly Internet Resource Collections
infomine.ucr.edu
> Supplies indexed and annotated links to more than ninety-five
> hundred databases and other resources of academic interest,
> grouped in interdisciplinary categories; also includes resources on
> using the Internet, maps, and teaching materials.

The Internet Public Library
www.ipl.org
> Selects worthwhile sources and organizes information by subject
> categories; a highly recommended site with many references,
> exhibits, and useful resources.

Librarians' Internet Index
www.lii.org
> Includes general reference information, topics of popular interest
> (as varied as automobiles, food, government, health, music, and
> recreation), and subjects ranging from the arts to world cultures.

News Index
www.newsindex.com
> Provides topic searches and access to the Web sites of 250 newspapers and periodicals.

RefDesk
www.refdesk.com
> Supplies access to reference materials, a variety of news organizations, and sites related to topics of current interest.

The Webliography: Internet Subject Guides
www.lib.lsu.edu/weblio.html
> Provides extensive annotated guides and access to academic and government resources in the humanities, sciences, and social sciences.

The WWW Virtual Library
www.vlib.org
> Provides links to information on a wide variety of topics.

3

Evaluating Sources
and Taking Notes

Your Working Bibliography

A working bibliography is a list of sources that you may ulti-
mately use for your project. As you find and begin to evaluate
research sources — articles, books, Web sites, and so on — you should
record source information for every source you think you might use.
(Relevant information includes everything you need to find the
source again and cite it correctly; the information you will need
varies based on the type of source, whether you found it in a library
or not, and whether you consulted it in print or online.) The emphasis here is on working because the list will probably include materials that end up not being useful. For this reason, you don't abso-
lutely need to put all entries into the documentation style you will
use (see Chapters 5–8). If you do follow the required documentation style, however, that part of your work will be done when you
prepare the final draft.

The following lists will help you keep track of the sorts of information you should try to find:

FOR A BOOK

Call number

Author(s) or editor(s)

Title and subtitle

Place of publication

Publisher

Year of publication

Other (translator, volume, edition)

FOR PART OF A BOOK

Call number

Author(s) of part

Title of part

Author(s) or editor(s) of book

Title of book

Place of publication

Publisher

Year of publication

Inclusive page numbers for part you are using

FOR A PERIODICAL ARTICLE

Call number of periodical

Author(s) of article

Title of article

Name of periodical

Volume number

Issue number

Date of issue

Inclusive page numbers for article

Database name and article identification number

FOR AN ELECTRONIC SOURCE

Author(s) (if available)

Title of document

Title of site

Editor(s) of site

Sponsor of site

Publication information for print version of source

Name of database or online service

Date of electronic publication or last update

Date you accessed the source

URL

For other kinds of sources (films, recordings, visuals), you should also list the information required by the documentation style you are using (see Chapters 5–8), and note where you found the information.

Evaluating Usefulness and Credibility

Since you want the information and ideas you glean from sources to be reliable and persuasive, you must evaluate each potential source

carefully. The following guidelines can help you assess the usefulness
and credibility of sources you are considering:

- *Your purpose.* What will this source add to your research project? Does
  it help you support a major point, demonstrate that you have thoroughly researched your topic, or help establish your own credibility
  through its authority?

- *Relevance.* How closely related is the source to the narrowed topic you
  are pursuing? You may need to read beyond the title and opening
  paragraph to check for relevance.

- *Level of specialization and audience.* General sources can be helpful as
  you begin your research, but you may then need the authority or
  currency of more specialized sources. On the other hand, extremely
  specialized works may be very hard to understand. Who was the
  source originally written for — the general public? experts in the
  field? advocates or opponents? How does this fit with your concept
  of your own audience?

- *Credentials of the publisher or sponsor.* What can you learn about the
  publisher or sponsor of the source you are using? For example, is it
  a major newspaper known for integrity in reporting, or is it a
  tabloid? Is it a popular source, whether in print or electronic, or is
  it sponsored by a professional organization or academic institution?
  If you're evaluating a book, is the publisher one you recognize or
  can find described on its own Web site? If you are evaluating a Web
  site, is the site's sponsor a commercial (.com), educational (.edu),
  governmental (.gov), military (.mil), network (.net), or nonprofit
  (.org) entity? No hard and fast rules exist for deciding what kind of
  source to use. But knowing the sponsor's or publisher's credentials
  can help you determine whether a source is appropriate for your
  research project.

- *Credentials of the author.* As you do your research, note names that
  come up from one source to another, since these references may
  indicate that the author is influential in the field. An author's
  credentials may also be presented in the article, book, or Web site, or
  you can search the Internet for information about the author. In
  U.S. academic writing, experts and those with significant experience
  in a field have more authority on the subject than others.

- *Date of publication.* Recent sources are often more useful than older ones, particularly in the sciences or other fields that change rapidly. However, in some fields — such as the humanities — the most authoritative works may be older ones. The publication dates of Internet sites can often be difficult to pin down. And even for sites that include dates of posting, remember that the material posted may have been composed sometime earlier. Most reliable will be those sites that list the dates of updating regularly.

- *Accuracy of the source.* How accurate and complete is the information in the source? How thorough is the bibliography or list of works cited that accompanies the source? Can you find other sources that corroborate what your source is saying?

- *Stance of the source.* Identify the source's point of view or rhetorical stance, and scrutinize it carefully. Does the source present facts, or does it interpret or evaluate them? If it presents facts, what is included and what is omitted, and why? If it interprets or evaluates information that is not disputed, the source's stance may be obvious, but at other times, you will need to think carefully about the source's goals. What does the author or sponsoring group want? to convince you of an idea? sell you something? call you to action in some way?

- *Cross-references to the source.* Is the source cited in other works? If you see your source cited by others, notice how they cite it and what they say about it to find additional clues to its credibility.

For more on evaluating Web sources and periodical articles, see the Source Maps on pp. 38–41.

Critical Reading and Interpretation

For those sources that you want to analyze more closely, reading with a critical eye can make your research process more efficient. Use the tips on pp. 37 and 42–43 to guide your critical reading.

GUIDELINES FOR EXAMINING POTENTIAL SOURCES

Looking quickly at the various parts of a source can provide useful information and help you decide whether to explore that particular source more thoroughly. You are already familiar with some of these basic elements: title and subtitle, title page and copyright page, home page, table of contents, index, footnotes, and bibliography. Be sure to check other items as well.

- *Abstracts* — concise summaries of articles and books — routinely precede journal articles and are often included in indexes and databases.

- A *preface* or *foreword* generally discusses the writer's purpose and thesis.

- *Subheadings* within the text can alert you to how much detail is given on a topic.

- A *conclusion* or *afterword* may summarize or draw the strands of an argument together.

- For an electronic source, click on some of the *links* to see if they're useful, and see if the overall *design* of the site is easy to navigate.

YOUR RESEARCH QUESTION

As you read, keep your research question in mind, and ask yourself the following questions:

- How does this material address your research question and support your hypothesis?
- What quotations from this source might help support your thesis?
- Does the source include counterarguments to your hypothesis that you will need to answer? If so, what answers can you provide?

SOURCE MAP: Evaluating Web Sources

Determine the credibility of the sponsoring organization.

(1) Consider the URL, specifically the top-level domain name. (For example, *.edu* may indicate that the sponsor is an accredited college or university; *.org* may indicate it's a nonprofit organization.) Ask yourself whether such a sponsor might be biased about the topic you're researching.

(2) Look for an *About* page or a link to the home page for background information on the sponsor, including a mission statement. What is the sponsoring organization's stance or point of view? Does the mission statement seem biased or balanced? Does the sponsor seem to take other points of view into account? What is the intended purpose of the site? Is this site meant to inform? Or is it trying to persuade, advertise, or accomplish something?

Determine the credibility of the author.

(3) Evaluate the author's credentials. On this Web page, the author appears to be a staff writer for the site. Although the author herself may not have a medical background, note that the article was reviewed by a physician and that it includes findings from a respected medical journal. If you suspect that an author may be biased, run a search on the author's name to find any affiliations with interest groups or any leaning toward one side of an issue. Ask yourself if the author seems qualified to write about the issue.

(4) Look for the date that indicates when the information was posted or last updated. Here, the date is given at the beginning of the article.

(5) Check to see if the sources referred to are also up-to-date. This author cites sources from July 2005. Ask yourself if, given your topic, an older source is acceptable or if only the most recent information will do.

Determine the accuracy of the information.

(6) How complete is the information in the source? Examine the works cited by the author. Are sources for statistics included? Do the sources cited seem credible? Is a list of additional resources provided? Here, the author cites the *New England Journal of Medicine* and the National Center for Complementary and Alternative Medicine in addition to two of WebMD's own articles. In some cases, it may be necessary to track down additional sources and corroborate what a source is saying.

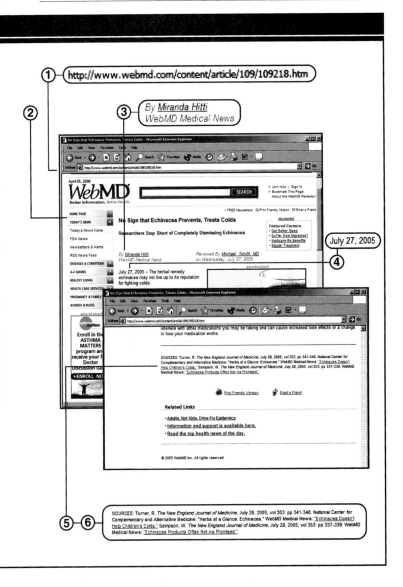

① http://www.webmd.com/content/article/109/109218.htm

③ By *Miranda Hitti*
WebMD Medical News

④ July 27, 2005

⑤ ⑥ SOURCES: Turner, R. *The New England Journal of Medicine*, July 28, 2005; vol 353: pp 341-348. National Center for Complementary and Alternative Medicine: "Herbs at a Glance: Echinacea." WebMD Medical News: "Echinacea Doesn't Help Children's Colds." Sampson, W. *The New England Journal of Medicine*, July 28, 2005; vol 353: pp 337-339. WebMD Medical News: "Echinacea Products Often Not As Promised."

SOURCE MAP: Evaluating Articles

Determine the relevance of the source.

(1) Look for an abstract, which provides a summary of the entire article. Is the source directly related to your research? Does it provide useful information and insights? Will your readers consider it persuasive support for your thesis?

Determine the credibility of the publication.

(2) Consider the publication's title. Words in the title such as *Journal, Review,* and *Quarterly* may indicate that the periodical is a scholarly source. Most research essays rely on authorities in a particular field, whose work usually appears in scholarly journals. For more on distinguishing between scholarly and popular sources, see p. 7.

(3) Try to determine the publisher or sponsor. This journal is published by Johns Hopkins University Press. Academic presses such as this one generally review articles carefully before publishing them and bear the authority of their academic sponsors.

Determine the credibility of the author.

(4) Evaluate the author's credentials. In this case, they are given in a note, which indicates that the author is a college professor and has written at least two books on related topics.

Determine the currency of the article.

(5) Look at the publication date and think about whether your topic and your credibility depend on your use of very current sources.

Determine the accuracy of the article.

(6) Look at the sources cited by the author of the article. Here, they are documented in footnotes. Ask yourself whether the works the author has cited seem credible and current. Are any of these works cited in other articles you've considered?

In addition, consider the following questions:

- What is the article's stance or point of view? What are the author's goals? What does the author want you to know or believe?

- How does this source fit in with your other sources? Does any of the information it provides contradict or challenge other sources?

HUMAN RIGHTS QUARTERLY

Prisons and Politics in Contemporary Latin America

Mark Ungar*

ABSTRACT

Despite democratization throughout Latin America, massive human rights abuses continue in the region's prisons. Conditions have become so bad that most governments have begun to enact improvements, including new criminal codes and facility decongestion. However, once in place, these reforms are undermined by chaotic criminal justice systems, poor policy administration, and rising crime rates leading to greater detention powers for the police. After describing current prison conditions in Latin America and the principal reforms to address them, this article explains how political and administrative limitations hinder the range of agencies and officials responsible for implementing those changes.

I. INTRODUCTION

Prison conditions not only constitute some of the worst human rights violations in contemporary Latin American democracies, but also reveal fundamental weaknesses in those democracies. Unlike most other human rights problems, those in the penitentiary system cannot be easily explained with authoritarian legacies or renegade officials. The systemic killing, overcrowding, disease, torture, rape, corruption, and due process abuses all occur under the state's twenty-four hour watch. Since the mid-1990s,

* *Mark Ungar* is Associate Professor of Political Science at Brooklyn College, City University of New York. Recent publications include the books *Elusive Reform: Democracy and the Rule of Law in Latin America* (Lynne Rienner, 2002) and *Violence and Politics: Globalization's Paradox* (Routledge, 2001) as well as articles and book chapters on democratization, policing, and judicial access. He works with Amnesty International USA and local rights groups in Latin America.

Human Rights Quarterly 25 (2003) 909–934 © 2003 by The Johns Hopkins University Press

The Johns Hopkins University Press

10.   Inspector General de Cárceles, Informe Anual (Caracas: Ministerio de Justicia 1994).
11.   *Overcrowding Main Cause of Riots in Latin American Prisons,* AFP, 30 Dec. 1997.
12.   Interviews with inmates, speaking on condition of anonymity in San Pedro prison (19 July 2000); Interviews with inmates, speaking on condition of anonymity in La Paz FELCN Prison (20 July 2000).
13.   Typhus, cholera, tuberculosis, and scabies run rampant and the HIV rate may be as high as 25 percent. The warden of Retén de la Planta, where cells built for one inmate house three or four, says the prisons "are collapsing" because of insufficient budgets to train personnel. "Things fall apart and stay that way." Interview, Luis A. Lara Roche, Warden of Retén de la Planta, Caracas, Venezuela, 19 May 1995. At El Dorado prison in Bolívar state, there is one bed for every four inmates, cells are infested with vermin, and inmates lack clean bathing water and eating utensils.
14.   *La Crisis Penitenciaria,* El Nacional (Caracas), 2 Sept. 1988, at D2. On file with author.

915

ezuela, the
jumped to
agency in
ers, far from
the number
mates form
PCC)—with
In the riots
began in
and spread
s—the PCC
CC leaders.
nd security
naffordable
rgest, some
tiny airless
tes living in
hose in the
az facility of
a Contra el
less cells of
able water,
th rats and
in weapons
ocaine and
on officials,
al Guard in
retribution.
s protesting
colony of El

THE AUTHOR'S STANCE AND TONE

Even a seemingly factual report, such as an encyclopedia article, is filled with judgments, often unstated. Read with an eye for the author's overall rhetorical stance, or perspective, as well as for facts or explicit opinions. Also pay attention to the author's tone, the way his or her attitude toward the topic and audience is conveyed. The following questions can help:

- Is the author a strong advocate or opponent of something? a skeptical critic? a specialist in the field?
- Are there any clues to why the author takes this stance? Is professional affiliation a factor?
- How does this stance affect the author's presentation and your reaction to it?
- What facts does the author include? Can you think of any important fact that is omitted?
- What is the author's tone? Is it cautious, angry, flippant, serious, impassioned? What words indicate this tone?

THE AUTHOR'S ARGUMENT AND EVIDENCE

Every piece of writing takes a position. Even a scientific report implicitly "argues" that we should accept it and its data as reliable. As you read, look for the main point or the main argument the author is making. Try to identify the reasons the author gives to support his or her position. Then try to determine *why* the author takes this position. Consider these questions:

- What is the author's main point, and what evidence supports it?
- How persuasive is the evidence? Can you think of a way to refute it?
- Can you detect any questionable logic or fallacious thinking?
- Does this author disagree with arguments you have read elsewhere? If so, what causes the disagreements—differences about facts or about how to interpret facts?

Synthesizing Sources

Your task as a reader is to identify and understand sources and sets of data as completely as possible. As a writer, your aim must be to present data and sources *to other readers* so that they can readily understand the point you are making. Doing so calls for you to notice patterns in your sources and to develop your own interpretation of them.

Throughout the research process, you are synthesizing — grouping similar pieces of data together, looking for patterns or trends, and identifying the gist, or main points, of the data. Doing so enables you to use your sources in pursuit of your own goals, rather than just stacking them up as unconnected bits of information. Often such synthesizing will lead you to make inferences — conclusions that are not explicitly stated but that follow logically from the data given.

Notes and Annotations

Note-taking methods vary greatly from one researcher to another, so you may decide to use a notebook, index cards, or a computer file. Regardless of the method, however, you should (1) record enough information to help you recall the major points of the source; (2) put the information in the form in which you are most likely to incorporate it into your research essay, whether a summary, a paraphrase, or a quotation; and (3) note all the information you will need to cite the source accurately. The following example shows the major items a note should include (numbered explanations are on p. 44):

ELEMENTS OF AN ACCURATE NOTE

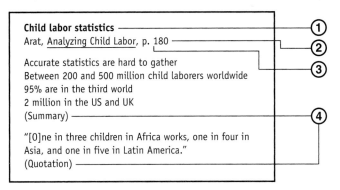

Child labor statistics — ①
Arat, <u>Analyzing Child Labor</u>, p. 180 — ②

Accurate statistics are hard to gather
Between 200 and 500 million child laborers worldwide — ③
95% are in the third world
2 million in the US and UK
(Summary) — ④

"[O]ne in three children in Africa works, one in four in Asia, and one in five in Latin America."
(Quotation)

(1) *Use a subject heading.* Label each note with a brief but descriptive subject heading so that you can group similar subtopics together.

(2) *Identify the source.* List the author's name and a shortened title of the source. Your working-bibliography entry for the source will contain the full bibliographic information, so you don't need to repeat it in each note.

(3) *Record exact page references (if available).* For online or other sources without page numbers, record the paragraph, screen, or other section number(s) if indicated.

(4) *Indicate whether the note is a direct quotation, paraphrase, or summary* (see below). Make sure quotations are copied accurately. Put square brackets around any change you make, and use ellipses if you omit material.

Taking complete notes will help you digest the source information as you read and incorporate the material into your text without inadvertently plagiarizing the source. Be sure to reread each note carefully, and recheck it against the source to make sure quotations, statistics, and specific facts are accurate.

The box below will help you determine whether to quote, paraphrase, or summarize various types of information. The guidelines that follow it offer note-taking strategies for all three types of notes.

KNOWING WHEN TO QUOTE, PARAPHRASE, OR SUMMARIZE

QUOTE

- wording that is so memorable or powerful or expresses a point so perfectly that you cannot change it without weakening the meaning you need

- authors' opinions you wish to emphasize

- authors' words that show you are considering varying perspectives

(Continued)

- respected authorities whose opinions support your ideas

- authors whose opinions challenge or vary greatly from those of others in the field

PARAPHRASE

- passages you do not wish to quote but whose details are important to your point

SUMMARIZE

- long passages whose main point is important to your point but whose details are not

Quotations

Some of the notes you take will contain quotations, which give the exact words of a source.

GUIDELINES FOR QUOTATIONS

- Copy quotations carefully, with punctuation, capitalization, and spelling *exactly* as in the original.

- Enclose the quotation in quotation marks; don't rely on your memory to distinguish your own words from those of the source.

- Use square brackets if you introduce words of your own into a quotation or make changes in it, and use ellipses if you omit material. If you later incorporate the quotation into your essay, copy it faithfully — brackets, ellipses, and all.

- Record the author's name, the shortened title, and the page number(s) on which the quotation appears. If the note refers

(Continued)

to more than one page, use a slash (/) within the quotation to indicate where one page ends and another begins. For sources without page numbers, record the paragraph, screen, or other section number(s), if any.

- Make sure you have a corresponding working-bibliography entry with complete source information.

- Label the note with a subject heading, and identify it as a quotation.

Paraphrases

A paraphrase accurately states all the relevant information from a passage *in your own words and sentence structures,* without any additional comments or elaborations. A paraphrase is useful when the main points of a passage, their order, and at least some details are important but—unlike passages worth quoting—the particular wording is not. Unlike a summary, a paraphrase always restates *all* the main points of a passage in the same order and often in about the same number of words.

GUIDELINES FOR PARAPHRASES

- Include all main points and any important details from the original source, in the same order in which the author presents them.

- State the meaning in your own words and sentence structures. If you want to include especially memorable language from the original, enclose it in quotation marks.

- Save your comments, elaborations, or reactions on another note.

- Record the author's name, the shortened title, and the page number(s) on which the original material appears. For sources

(Continued)

without page numbers, record the paragraph, screen, or other section number(s), if any.

- Make sure you have a corresponding working-bibliography entry with complete source information.

- Label the note with a subject heading, and identify it as a paraphrase.

Summaries

A summary is a significantly shortened version of a passage or even of a whole chapter or work that captures main ideas *in your own words*. Unlike a paraphrase, a summary uses just enough information to record the main points you wish to emphasize. Your goal is to keep the summary as brief as possible, capturing only the main idea of the original and not distorting the author's meaning.

GUIDELINES FOR SUMMARIES

- Include just enough information to recount the main points you wish to cite. A summary is usually far shorter than the original.

- Use your own words. If you include any language from the original, enclose it in quotation marks.

- Record the author's name, the shortened title, and the page number(s) on which the original material appears. For sources without page numbers, record the paragraph, screen, or other section number(s), if any.

- Make sure you have a corresponding working-bibliography entry with complete source information.

- Label the note with a subject heading, and identify it as a summary.

4

Acknowledging Sources and Avoiding Plagiarism

Which Sources to Acknowledge

As you carry out research, you should understand the distinction between materials that require acknowledgment and those that do not.

Materials That Do Not Require Acknowledgment

Information does not need to be credited to a source if it is well known or if you gathered the data yourself.

- *Common knowledge.* If most readers know a fact, you probably do not need to cite a source for it. You do not need to credit a source to say that George Bush was reelected in 2004, for example.
- *Facts available in a wide variety of sources.* If a number of encyclopedias, almanacs, reputable Web sites, or textbooks include a certain piece of information, you usually need not cite a specific source for it. For instance, you would not need to cite a source if you write that the Japanese bombed Pearl Harbor on December 7, 1941.

- *Findings from field research.* If you conduct observations or surveys, announce your findings as your own. Acknowledge people you interview as individuals rather than as part of a survey.

If you are not sure whether a fact, an observation, or a piece of information requires acknowledgment, err on the side of safety, and cite the source.

Materials That Require Acknowledgment

For material that does not fall under the preceding categories, credit sources as fully as possible. Follow the conventions of the citation style you are using (see Chapters 5–8), and include each source in a bibliography or list of works cited.

- *Quotations, paraphrases, and summaries.* Whenever you use another person's words, ideas, or opinions, credit the source. Even though the wording of a paraphrase or summary is your own, you should still acknowledge the source.

- *Facts that aren't widely known or claims that are arguable.* If your readers would be unlikely to know a fact, or if an author presents as fact a claim that may or may not be true, cite the source. To claim, for instance, that Switzerland is amassing an offensive nuclear arsenal would demand the citation of a source because Switzerland has long been an officially neutral state. If you are not sure whether a fact will be familiar to your readers or whether a statement is arguable, go ahead and cite the source.

- *Images, statistics, charts, tables, graphs, and other visuals from any source.* Credit all visual and statistical material not derived from your own field research, even if you create your own graph or table from the data provided in a source.

- *Help provided by others.* If an instructor gave you a good idea or if friends responded to your draft or helped you conduct surveys, give credit — usually in a footnote that says something like "Thanks to Kiah Williams, who first suggested this connection."

Here is a quick-reference chart to guide you in deciding whether or not you need to acknowledge a source:

NEED TO ACKNOWLEDGE	DON'T NEED TO ACKNOWLEDGE
quotations	your own words, observations, surveys, and so on
paraphrases or summaries of a source	common knowledge
ideas you glean from a source	facts available in many sources
facts that aren't widely known	drawings or other visuals you create on your own
graphs, tables, and other statistical information from a source	
photographs, visuals, video, or sound taken from sources	
experiments conducted by others	
interviews that are not part of a survey	
organization or structure taken from a source	
help or advice from an instructor or another student	

Academic Integrity and Plagiarism

The principle of academic integrity in intellectual work allows you to trust the sources you use and to demonstrate that your own work is equally trustworthy. While there are many ways to damage academic integrity, two that are especially important are inaccurate or incomplete citation of sources — also called unintentional plagiarism — and plagiarism that is deliberately intended to pass off one writer's work as another's.

Inaccurate or Incomplete Citation of Sources

If your paraphrase is too close to the original wording or sentence structure of the source (even if you identify the source); if you do not identify the source of a quotation (even if you include the quotation marks); or if you fail to indicate clearly the source of an idea that you obviously did not come up with on your own, you may be accused of plagiarism even if your intent was not to plagiarize. Inaccurate or incomplete acknowledgment of sources often results either from carelessness or from not learning how to borrow material properly in the first place. Still, because the costs of even unintentional plagiarism can be severe, it's important to understand how it can happen and how you can guard against it.

As a writer of academic integrity, you will want to take responsibility for your research and for acknowledging all sources accurately. One easy way to keep track is to keep photocopies or printouts as you do your research; then you can identify needed quotations right on each copy.

Deliberate Plagiarism

Deliberate plagiarism — handing in an essay written by a friend or purchased (or simply downloaded) from an essay-writing company; cutting and pasting passages directly from source materials without marking them with quotation marks and acknowledging your sources; failing to credit the source of an idea or concept in your text — is what most people think of when they hear the word plagiarism. This form of plagiarism is particularly troubling because it represents dishonesty and deception: those who intentionally plagiarize present the hard thinking and hard work of someone else as their own, and they deceive readers by claiming knowledge they don't really have.

Deliberate plagiarism is also fairly simple to spot: your instructor will be well acquainted with your writing and likely to notice any sudden shifts in the style or quality of your work. In addition, by typing a few words from an essay into a search engine, your instructor can identify "matches" very easily.

AVOIDING PLAGIARISM

- Maintain an accurate and thorough working bibliography.

- Establish a consistent note-taking system, listing sources and page numbers and clearly identifying all quotations, paraphrases, summaries, statistics, and visuals.

- Identify all quotations with quotation marks—both in your notes and in your essay.

- Be sure your summaries and paraphrases use your own words and sentence structures.

- Give a citation or note for each quotation, paraphrase, summary, arguable assertion or opinion, statistic, and visual from a source, including an online source.

- Prepare an accurate and complete list of sources cited according to the required documentation style. (See Chapters 5 through 8.)

- Plan ahead on writing assignments so that you can avoid the temptation to take shortcuts.

5

Research in the Humanities

Resources in the Humanities

INDEXES AND DATABASES FOR THE HUMANITIES

Arts and Humanities Citation Index. Covers 1975–. Indexes citations in articles from over a thousand periodicals in the humanities and arts; entries allow tracing influence through later citations of books and periodicals. (online)

Essay and General Literature Index. Covers 1900–. Indexes authors and subjects of separate essays published in collections. (Essays are not usually listed separately in library catalogs.) (online)

Humanities Index. Covers 1984–. Formerly *Social Sciences and Humanities Index,* 1965–1974, and *International Index,* 1907–1965. Indexes and abstracts articles and book reviews from about three hundred periodicals covering literature, history, the arts, the classics, and other topics in the humanities. (online)

WEB RESOURCES FOR THE HUMANITIES

EDSITEment
www.edsitement.neh.gov
    Links to nearly two hundred high-quality humanities Web sites, selected under the auspices of the National Endowment for the Humanities.

Infomine: Scholarly Internet Resource Collections
www.infomine.ucr.edu
> Supplies indexed and annotated links to databases and other resources of academic interest in the humanities, performing arts, and visual arts.

Voice of the Shuttle: Web Page for Humanities Research
www.vos.ucsb.edu
> Includes highlights, top sites, and links to extensiveResearch Essay resources for general or specialized research in the humanities.

The Webliography: Internet Subject Guides
www.lib.lsu.edu/subjectguides/humanities.html
> Provides extensive annotated guides to Web resources in many fields in the humanities, including art, film, theater, literature, history, music, classics, and others.

Art and Architecture

GENERAL REFERENCE SOURCES FOR ART AND ARCHITECTURE

Encyclopedia of Architecture: Design, Engineering, and Construction. 5 vols. 1988–1990. Supplies articles, including bibliographies, on architectural history, technology, construction, and design.

Encyclopedia of Artists. 6 vols. 2000. Provides an illustrated introduction to Western art, with entries on artists, works, and major periods from the Middle Ages through the present.

Encyclopedia of World Art. 15 vols., plus supplements. 1959–1968; 1983; 1987. Includes articles, many illustrated, on artists, art history, art in other cultures and societies, and related topics.

The Grove Dictionary of Art. 34 vols. 1996. Examines all the visual arts except film, with fifteen thousand illustrations.

McGraw-Hill Dictionary of Art. 1969. Supplies definitions and longer articles, including illustrations.

Oxford Dictionary of Art. 2004. Provides entries on the Western fine and decorative arts, including artists, terms, and institutions. (online)

INDEXES AND DATABASES FOR
ART AND ARCHITECTURE

ARTBibliographies Modern. Covers 1969–. Lists and abstracts articles, books, and catalogs about art. (online)

Art Index. Covers 1929–. *Art Index Retrospective* covers 1929–1984. Indexes articles from about 250 periodicals on the fine arts, archaeology, architecture, interior design, city planning, photography, film, and other topics. (online)

Avery Index to Architectural Periodicals. Covers 1741–. Available in print and online. Contains citations to articles in architecture and design, archaeology, city planning, interior design, and historic preservation.

BHA: Bibliography of the History of Art. Covers 1973–. Last print edition, 1999. Formerly *RILA (Répertoire internationale de la littérature de l'art),* 1975–1989, and *RAA (Répertoire d'art et d'archéologie),* 1910–1963. Lists articles from about four thousand periodicals plus books, papers, and other materials about the arts. (online as *Art Literature International*)

Fine Arts: A Bibliographic Guide to Basic Reference Works, Historics, and Handbooks. 1990. Lists and annotates references to resources in the fine arts.

Grove Art Online A continuously updated online version of *The Dictionary of Art* (34 vols., 1996) and *The Oxford Companion to Western Art* (2001); includes articles on artists, movements, and works in the fine and decorative arts worldwide, as well as image links and a search engine.

WEB RESOURCES FOR ART AND ARCHITECTURE

Architecture and Building
library.nevada.edu/arch/rsrce/webrsrce/contents.html
Organizes extensive topical and alphabetical listings of Web resources on architecture and related issues.

The Art History Research Centre
www.harmsen.net/ahrc
Introduces Internet research in art history and links to many resources such as Internet art collections, library catalogs, periodical indexes, newsgroups, and other art history servers.

Art History Resources on the Web
witcombe.sbc.edu/ARTHLinks.html
> Provides an extraordinarily detailed set of chronologically organized links to art history sources, from prehistoric through modern.

Art Museum Network
www.amn.org
> Free access to information about collections, exhibitions, and services of the world's largest and most prestigious art museums.

The Getty Information Institute
www.getty.edu/research
> Provides access to major databases and indexes on art and cultural history, including specialized search tools and numerous graphic images with reference pages.

History of Art Virtual Library
www.chart.ac.uk/vlib
> Includes links to art history sites, museums, galleries, art history organizations, and university art departments.

National Gallery of Art
www.nga.gov/
> Supplies images from the collection and news about current displays and educational opportunities.

Virtual Library Museums Pages
vlmp.museophile.com
> Includes a large number of links to recent and current exhibitions at many major museums, by country.

World Art Treasures
www.bergerfoundation.ch/
> Offers in-depth links to selected artists' works and areas of art, with good links to other sites.

World Wide Arts Resources
world-arts-resources.com/
> Contains extensive links and search capability to artists, art history, museums, and other art-related topics.

The WWW Virtual Library—Architecture
www.clr.toronto.edu/VIRTUALLIB/arch.html
> Supplies links to varied resources on architecture, landscape architecture, architectural engineering, and related topics.

The WWW Virtual Library—Art
www.icom.org/vlmp/galleries.html
> Provides an excellent collection of links to both art and literature sites, including links to other virtual libraries.

Classics

GENERAL REFERENCE SOURCES FOR THE CLASSICS

The Oxford Classical Dictionary. 2003. Supplies articles with bibliographies on classical figures, literature, places, and events. (online)

The Oxford Companion to Classical Civilization. 2004. Includes articles on classical writers, major works and characters, literary forms, and mythology, as well as background information on classical history, geography, religion, politics, and social context. (online)

INDEXES AND DATABASES FOR THE CLASSICS

L'Année Philologique. Covers 1928–. Indexes periodical articles, books, and other resources about classical language, literature, history, law, science, culture, and other topics. (online)

WEB RESOURCES FOR THE CLASSICS

Classics and Mediterranean Archaeology
www.gzg.fn.bw.schule.de/faecher/links/classic.html
> Provides links to widely varied resources on texts, field sites, projects, images, archaeological excavations, exhibitions, museums, academic institutions, maps, publications, and other information on classical studies.

Classics at Oxford
www.classics.ox.ac.uk/resources/index.html
> Provides links to many resources in the classics and ancient history; has search capability.

The Perseus Digital Library
www.perseus.tufts.edu
> Supplies extensive information on the ancient world, including background information, Greek texts and translations, maps, descriptions, and over thirteen thousand images of vases, coins, buildings, sculptures, and site plans.

History

GENERAL REFERENCE SOURCES FOR HISTORY

The Cambridge Ancient History. 19 vols. 2006. Includes articles, illustrations, maps, and other supporting materials in volumes on early civilization in Europe and the Middle East; additional volumes supply illustrations and appendices.

The Cambridge Encyclopedia of Latin America and the Caribbean. 1992. Supplies articles on the history, politics, economics, and culture of the region.

The Cambridge History of Africa. 8 vols. 1986. Covers African history chronologically from early times through the mid-1970s. (online)

The Cambridge Medieval History. 9 vols. 1999. Covers the major events and changes in medieval history, including government, religion, and cultural background.

Chambers Dictionary of World History. 2005. Contains over seventy-five hundred entries on key figures and events of world history, with an in-depth focus on the period between AD 1000 and 2000; includes maps, tables, and family trees.

Dictionary of Concepts in History. 1986. Supplies articles on major historical concepts, including definitions, histories of the concepts, and additional sources of information.

Dictionary of the Middle Ages. 13 vols. 1982–1989, with 2004 supplement. Provides authoritative articles with bibliographies on many people and topics relating to the culture, politics, and religion of the medieval period (AD 500–1500).

Encyclopedia of American Social History. 3 vols. 1993. Includes articles and bibliographies on aspects of ordinary life, work, and leisure.

Encyclopedia of Asian History. 4 vols. 1988. Supplies articles, often with bibliographies for further research in English, including major figures and wide-ranging topics about Asian history and civilization from early times on.

Encyclopedia of the Renaissance. 1999. Offers brief entries on the Renaissance, including historical, political, and other topics.

Encyclopedia of World History. 1999. Contains entries on events, figures, and concepts from prehistoric through modern times; includes cross-references, maps, portraits, and engravings.

The Oxford Companion to British History. 2002. Provides entries on social, political, cultural, economic, and scientific events, both national and local, from 55 BCE to the 1990s; includes maps and genealogical charts. (online)

The Oxford Companion to United States History. 2004. Examines major figures, events, ideologies, and developments in technology, the economy, immigration, and urbanization from before 1492 to the end of the twentieth century. (online)

The Oxford Dictionary of World History. 2003. Covers key figures, subjects, and events from prehistoric to modern times in concise entries; includes detailed maps on particular events and topics. (online)

United States History: A Selective Guide to Information Sources. 1994. Offers a topically arranged annotated list of the reference works published in the previous two hundred years on the subject of U.S. history, including print sources, online databases, and CD-ROMs.

INDEXES AND DATABASES FOR HISTORY

America: History and Life. 1964–2005. Formerly in *History Abstracts* (1954–1963). Indexes and abstracts articles from more than two thousand periodicals on the history and culture of North America (United States and Canada), including local, regional, and national coverage. (online)

Handbook for Research in American History: A Guide to Bibliographies and Other Reference Books. 1994. Lists reference sources covering many aspects of American history.

Harvard Guide to American History. 2 vols. 1974. Supplies research guidance and lists major sources about notable people and topics as diverse as social context, religion, and law; vol. 2 chronologically surveys U.S. history.

Historical Abstracts. 1954–2005. Indexes and abstracts articles from more than two thousand periodicals and books on history, culture, historical research methods, and regional, national, and worldwide topics from 1450 on, excluding North America. (online)

Reference Sources in History: An Introductory Guide. 2004. Lists and annotates resources for studying history worldwide in all periods. (online)

WEB RESOURCES FOR HISTORY

Bedford/St. Martin's: Make History
bedfordstmartins.com/history
Provides an annotated list of links to history sites.

Eurodocs
eurodocs.lib.byu.edu/index.php/Main_Page
Offers primary historical documents from western Europe; organized by country.

Gateway to World History
www.history.ccsu.edu/History_web_links.htm
Supports searches for teachers and students of world history, and allows links to more specific areas.

Historical Text Archive
historicaltextarchive.com/
Provides access to many world history texts; organized by both area and topic.

The History Net
www.theHistoryNet.com/
A project of the National Historical Society; provides a historical magazine as well as a search service.

Internet History Sourcebooks Project
www.fordham.edu/halsall
Collections of public domain and copy-permitted historical texts for educational use.

The Library of Congress: American Memory
memory.loc.gov
An extensive site with text and links to millions of primary-source items (including maps, photos, and documents) from the Library of Congress and other collections; has excellent search capabilities.

World History Archives
www.hartford-hwp.com/archives/
> Offers access to actual versions of important texts in world history and many links to contemporary writings.

The WWW Virtual Library—History
vlib.iue.it/history
> Provides links to history servers by subject research, eras and epochs, historical topics, and countries and regions; includes search capability.

Literature

GENERAL REFERENCE SOURCES FOR LITERATURE

The Cambridge History of American Literature. 2006–. Covers poetry, prose, and literary criticism from 1590 to the present in multiple volumes that include thematically arranged entries on works of writers, critics, and scholars.

Dictionary of Literary Biography. 25 vols. 1978–. Supplies articles, including bibliographies and photographs, on the major writers representing each period or topic covered. (online)

Encyclopedia of Folklore and Literature. 1998. Includes entries about authors, works, scholars, and movements of folklore and literature throughout the world. (online)

Encyclopedia of the Novel. 2 vols. 1998. Focuses on the development of the novel throughout the world and includes over six hundred essays on writers and novels, as well as regional histories of the novel. (online)

Harper Handbook to Literature. 1997. Provides a dictionary of literary terms, concepts, genres, and movements with a mixture of brief entries and longer entries with bibliographies.

The Oxford Companion to American Literature. 1995. Supplies articles on authors, works, characters, and other literary topics, as well as on related background topics.

The Oxford Companion to English Literature. 2006. Supplies articles on literary topics, terms, authors, works, characters, movements, trends, and influences. (online)

Reader's Guide to Literature in English. 1996. Includes entries on writers, literary devices, genres, movements, criticism, and the literatures of various groups, regions, and time periods. (online)

INDEXES AND DATABASES FOR LITERATURE

MLA International Bibliography of Books and Articles on the Modern Languages and Literature. Covers 1880s–. 5 vols. 1921–. Indexes articles from over three thousand periodicals plus books and dissertations on literature and language, including literary works, authors, national literatures, literary movements and themes, literary theory and criticism, linguistics, and related topics. (online)

Reference Works in British and American Literature. 2 vols. 1998. Lists and annotates publications and other resources for studying literary topics and specific authors. (online)

WEB RESOURCES FOR LITERATURE

In Other Words: A Lexicon of the Humanities
www.sil.org/humanities/
> Provides an interesting hyperlinked lexicon and glossary of major terms in literary criticism, rhetoric, and linguistics.

International Gay and Lesbian Review
www.one.institute.org
> Provides abstracts and reviews of many books related to lesbian, gay, bisexual, and transgender studies.

Literary Resources on the Net
newark.rutgers.edu/~jlynch/lit/
> Allows you to search for online literary materials and provides a list of periodicals and genre-based categories to explore.

New American Studies Web
www.georgetown.edu/crossroads/asw/
> Provides links to many elements of American studies, with an emphasis on literary texts, authors, approaches, genres, and associations.

Project Gutenberg Master Index
promo.net/pg

Offers the best current index to PG texts, most of which are now in the public domain.

Resources for Russian and Slavic Languages and Literature
www.library.vanderbilt.edu/central/russian.html
Provides links to Web sites, dictionaries, literary sites, e-journals, e-texts, departments, and professional organizations.

Romance Languages Resources Page
humanities.uchicago.edu/depts/romance/resources.html
Offers links to cultural and textual resources and to sites that help those studying romance languages.

Music

GENERAL REFERENCE SOURCES FOR MUSIC

The New Grove Dictionary of Music and Musicians. 29 vols. 2001. Supplies entries on thousands of musicians and music topics, including bibliographies, lists of works, maps, family trees, and illustrations of instruments. (online)

The New Oxford Companion to Music. 2 vols. 1983. Provides entries defining musical terms, types of music, aspects of music history, and related topics.

New Oxford History of Music. 10 vols. 1954–2001. Covers music, ancient through modern, including bibliographies and music examples.

INDEXES AND DATABASES FOR MUSIC

Music: A Guide to the Reference Literature. 1987. Supplies annotated lists of reference sources about music, including bibliographies, discographies, periodicals, and music organizations.

Music Index: A Subject-Author Guide to Current Music Periodical Literature. 1949–. Indexes articles from over three hundred periodicals on music and musicians. (CD-ROM)

Music Reference and Research Materials: An Annotated Bibliography. 1997. Lists standard reference sources about music.

RILM Abstracts of Music Literature. 1966–. Indexes and abstracts articles, books, and other sources. (online)

WEB RESOURCES FOR MUSIC

Classical Music on the Web
classicalusa.com
> Offers an "organized jumpstation" to the best classical music sites on the Web.

Music Libraries
hcl.harvard.edu/libraries/#loebmusic
> Contains links, with search capability, to databases, journals, and many other music-related sites.

Sibelius Academy Music Resources
www.siba.fi/kulttuuripalvelut/music.html
> Provides links to every aspect of music appreciation, production, and education.

Worldwide Internet Music Resources
www.music.indiana.edu/music_resources/
> Includes a general list of links to musicians, composers, performance sites, genres, research, industry, and journals.

Philosophy and Religion

**GENERAL REFERENCE SOURCES FOR
PHILOSOPHY AND RELIGION**

The Cambridge Dictionary of Philosophy. 1999. Surveys key concepts and figures in both Western and non-Western philosophy, with extensive coverage of contemporary philosophers and new fields of thought.

Dictionary of Philosophy. 1996. Supplies entries on key terms and notable philosophers.

Encyclopedia of Philosophy. 4 vols. 1973. Includes articles and bibliographies on philosophers and topics of significance in the field.

Encyclopedia of Religion. 16 vols. 2005. Provides articles and bibliographies on both historical and present-day religions worldwide, including beliefs, practices, and major figures and groups. (online)

The Routledge Encyclopedia of Philosophy. 10 vols. 2000. Contains entries on concepts, scholarship, schools, and themes of world philosophy and religion. (online)

**INDEXES AND DATABASES FOR
PHILOSOPHY AND RELIGION**

Philosopher's Index. 1967–. Indexes and abstracts books and articles from
about three hundred periodicals. (online)

Philosophy: A Guide to the Reference Literature. 2006. Supplies annotated
entries on reference works in philosophy. (online)

Religion Index One: Periodicals; Religion Index Two: Multi-Author Works. 1949–.
Annual. Indexes and abstracts books and articles from several hundred periodicals. (online as ATLA Religion Database)

Religious and Theological Abstracts. Covers 1958–. Indexes and abstracts articles from several hundred periodicals. (online)

Religious Information Sources: A Worldwide Guide. 1992. Lists sources for all
world religions.

WEB RESOURCES FOR PHILOSOPHY AND RELIGION

American Philosophical Association Home Page
www.apa.udel.edu/apa/index.html
    Includes Web resources with guides to philosophy, philosophers,
    texts, journals, and academic organizations.

Guide to Philosophy on the Internet
www.earlham.edu/~peters/philinks.htm
    Includes links to sites with philosophy guides (in various languages),
    philosophers, journals, organizations, dictionaries, and many topics
    dealing with philosophy.

Hippias: Limited Area Search of Philosophy on the Internet
www.iep.utm.edu/h/hippias.htm
    Provides keyword searches as well as links to associated sites and
    search tools.

Religion and Philosophy Resources on the Internet
www.bu.edu/sth/sthlibrary/guides/index.html
    Offers selected annotated links to resources on philosophy and reli-
    gion, including Christianity, Judaism, Islam, and Asian religions.

Religion (Humanities): Galaxy
www.galaxy.com/directory/22694

Supplies access to collections of resources and directories for the study of religion.

The WWW Virtual Library—Philosophy
www.bristol.ac.uk/philosophy/department/resources/virtual.html
   Provides links to thousands of sources, including articles, journals, books, databases, and discussion groups; allows searches.

Theater and Film

GENERAL REFERENCE SOURCES FOR THEATER AND FILM

The Concise Oxford Companion to the Theatre. 1992. Supplies essays on theater history and style, buildings, dramatists, performers, directors, festivals, and technology. (online)

Film Encyclopedia. 2005. Supplies biographical and topical entries on many aspects of film. (online)

McGraw-Hill Encyclopedia of World Drama. 5 vols. 1984. Supplies extensive articles, including bibliographies, on playwrights, theaters, genres, dramatic terms, regional drama, and related topics.

INDEXES AND DATABASES FOR THEATER AND FILM

Film Literature Index. Covers 1976–. Indexes articles from several hundred periodicals on film, television, and video. (online)

International Index to Film Periodicals. Covers 1972–. Indexes articles, interviews, and reviews from more than eighty-five periodicals, with entries divided into three sections: general subjects, individual films, and biography. (online)

WEB RESOURCES FOR THEATER AND FILM

McCoy's Brief Guide to Internet Resources in Theatre and Performance Studies
www.stetson.edu/departments/csata/thr_guid.html
   Supplies useful research resources on topics such as acting, stagecraft, playwrights, and plays, as well as an annotated list of especially helpful sites.

Playbill Online
www.playbill.com
> Covers theater news, awards, and listings, and provides links through Theatre Central to a directory of resources on playwrights, stagecraft, Shakespeare, theater companies, casting calls, publications, and other varied topics.

Theatre Resources at ELAC (East Los Angeles College)
www.perspicacity.com
> Includes a wide range of resources on plays, playwrights, characters, costumes, acting, directing, and other topics, with links to other sites.

World Wide Arts Resources: Theater
wwar.com.categories/Theater
> Provides numerous links, by category, to most aspects of theater, including acting, choreography, plays, Broadway theater, and opera; has search capability.

The WWW Virtual Library: Theatre and Drama
vl-theatre.com
> Provides international theater resources (including studies, collections of images, events, companies, and academic institutions) and also indexes plays available online.

MLA Style

This section discusses the Modern Language Association (MLA) style of formatting manuscripts and documenting sources, which is widely used in literature, languages, and other fields in the humanities.

For more information on the Modern Language Association style, consult the *MLA Handbook for Writers of Research Papers,* Sixth Edition (2003).

In-Text Citations

MLA style requires documentation in the text of an essay for every quotation, paraphrase, summary, or other material that must be cited. In-text citations document material from other sources with both signal phrases and parenthetical references. Signal phrases introduce the material, often including the author's name. Parenthetical references direct you to full bibliographic entries in a list of works cited at the end of the text.

Keep your parenthetical references short, but include enough information in the parentheses to allow readers to locate the full citation in the works-cited list. Place a parenthetical reference as near the relevant material as possible without disrupting the flow of the sentence. Note in the following examples *where* punctuation is placed in relation to the parentheses. Except for block quotations, place any punctuation mark *after* the closing parenthesis. If you are referring to a quotation, place the parenthetical reference *after* the closing quotation mark but *before* any other punctuation mark. For block quotations, place the reference one space after the final punctuation mark.

DIRECTORY TO MLA STYLE FOR IN-TEXT CITATIONS

1. AUTHOR NAMED IN A SIGNAL PHRASE

Ordinarily, you can use the author's name in a signal phrase that introduces the material and cite the page number(s) in parentheses. You may want to use the full name the first time you cite a source, but use just the last name for later references.

Herrera indicates that Kahlo believed in a "vitalistic form of pantheism" (328).

2. AUTHOR NAMED IN A PARENTHETICAL REFERENCE

When you do not mention the author in a signal phrase, include the author's last name before the page number(s) in the parentheses. Use no punctuation between the author's name and the page number(s).

In places, Beauvoir "sees Marxists as believing in subjectivity" (Whitmarsh 63).

3. TWO OR THREE AUTHORS

Use all the authors' last names in a signal phrase or parenthetical reference.

Gortner, Hebrun, and Nicolson maintain that "opinion leaders" influence other people in an organization because they are respected, not because they hold high positions (175).

4. FOUR OR MORE AUTHORS

Use the names of all authors or the first author's name and *et al.* ("and others") in a signal phrase or parenthetical reference.

As Belenky, Clinchy, Goldberger, and Tarule assert, examining the lives of women expands our understanding of human development (7).

5. ORGANIZATION AS AUTHOR

Give the organization's full name or a shortened form of it in a signal phrase or parenthetical reference.

Any study of social welfare involves a close analysis of "the impacts, the benefits, and the costs" of its policies (Social Research Corporation iii).

6. UNKNOWN AUTHOR

Use the full title of the work or a shortened version in a signal phrase or parenthetical reference.

"Hype," by one analysis, is "an artificially engendered atmosphere of hysteria" ("Today's Marketplace" 51).

7. AUTHOR OF TWO OR MORE WORKS CITED IN THE SAME PROJECT

If your list of works cited has more than one work by the same author, give the title of the work you are citing or a shortened version in a signal phrase or parenthetical reference.

Gardner shows readers their own silliness in his description of a "pointless, ridiculous monster, crouched in the shadows, stinking of dead men, murdered children, and martyred cows" (Grendel 2).

8. TWO OR MORE AUTHORS WITH THE SAME LAST NAME

Include the author's first *and* last names in a signal phrase or first initial and last name in a parenthetical reference.

Children will learn to write if they are allowed to choose their own subjects, James Britton asserts, citing the Schools Council study of the 1960s (37-42).

9. MULTIVOLUME WORK

In a parenthetical reference, note the volume number first and then the page number(s), with a colon and one space between them.

> Modernist writers prized experimentation and gradually even sought to blur the line between poetry and prose, according to Forster (3: 150).

If you name only one volume of the work in your list of works cited, include only the page number in the parentheses.

10. LITERARY WORK

Literary works are often available in many different editions. For a prose work, cite the page number(s) from the edition you used followed by a semicolon, and then give other identifying information that will lead readers to the passage in any edition. Indicate the act and/or scene in a play (*37; sc. 1*). For a novel, indicate the part or chapter (*175; ch. 4*).

> Dostoyevsky's character Mitya wonders aloud about the "terrible tragedies realism inflicts on people" (376; bk. 8, ch. 2).

For a poem, instead of page numbers cite the part (if there is one) and line(s), separated by a period. If you are citing only line numbers, use the word *line(s)* in the first reference (*lines 33–34*).

> Whitman speculates, "All goes onward and outward, nothing collapses, / And to die is different from what any one supposed, and luckier" (6.129-30).

For a verse play, give only the act, scene, and line numbers, separated by periods.

> As Macbeth begins, the witches greet Banquo as "Lesser than Macbeth, and greater" (1.3.65).

11. WORK IN AN ANTHOLOGY

For an essay, short story, or other piece of prose reprinted in an anthology, use the name of the author of the work, not the editor of the anthology, but use the page number(s) from the anthology.

Narratives of captivity play a major role in early writing by women in the United States, as Silko demonstrates (219).

12. SACRED TEXT

To cite a sacred text such as the Qur'an or the Bible, give the title of the edition you used, followed by location information, such as the book, chapter, and verse, separated by a period. In your text, spell out the names of books. In parenthetical references, use abbreviations for books with names of five or more letters (*Gen.* for *Genesis*).

He ignored the admonition "Pride goes before destruction, and a haughty spirit before a fall" (New Oxford Annotated Bible, Prov. 16.18).

13. INDIRECT SOURCE

Use the abbreviation *qtd. in* to indicate that you are quoting from someone else's report of a conversation, interview, letter, or the like.

Arthur Miller says, "When somebody is destroyed everybody finally contributes to it, but in Willy's case, the end product would be virtually the same" (qtd. in Martin and Meyer 375).

14. TWO OR MORE SOURCES IN ONE CITATION

Separate the information with semicolons.

Some economists recommend that employment be redefined to include unpaid domestic labor (Clark 148; Nevins 39).

15. ENTIRE WORK OR ONE-PAGE ARTICLE

Include the reference in the text without any page numbers or parentheses.

Michael Ondaatje's poetic sensibility transfers beautifully to prose in The English Patient.

16. WORK WITHOUT PAGE NUMBERS

If a work has no page numbers or is only one page long, you may omit the page number. If a work uses paragraph numbers instead, use the abbreviation *par.* (or *pars.*). If a parenthetical reference to a work with paragraph numbers includes the author's name, use a comma after the name.

Whitman considered their speech "a source of a native grand opera" (Ellison, par. 13).

17. ELECTRONIC OR NONPRINT SOURCE

Give enough information in a signal phrase or parenthetical reference for readers to locate the source in the list of works cited. Usually use the author or title under which you list the source. Specify a source's page, section, paragraph, or screen numbers, if numbered, in parentheses.

Kilgore, the bloodthirsty lieutenant colonel played by Robert Duvall, declares, "I love the smell of napalm in the morning" (Apocalypse Now).

As a Slate analysis has noted, "Prominent sports psychologists get praised for their successes and don't get grief for their failures" (Engber).

MLA Format for Explanatory and Bibliographic Notes

MLA style recommends explanatory notes for information or commentary that would not readily fit into your text but is needed for clarification or further explanation. In addition, MLA style permits bibliographic notes for citing several sources for one point and for offering thanks to, information about, or evaluation of a source. Use superscript numbers in the text to refer readers to the notes, which may appear as endnotes (typed under the heading *Notes* on a separate page after the text but before the list of works cited) or as footnotes at the bottom of the page (typed four lines below the last text line).

SUPERSCRIPT NUMBER IN TEXT

Stewart emphasizes the existence of social contacts in Hawthorne's life so that the audience will accept a different Hawthorne, one more attuned to modern times than the figure in Woodberry.[3]

NOTE

[3] Woodberry does, however, show that Hawthorne was often an unsociable individual. He emphasizes the seclusion of Hawthorne's mother, who separated herself from her family after the death of her husband, often even taking meals alone (28). Woodberry seems to imply that Mrs. Hawthorne's isolation rubbed off onto her son.

MLA Format for a List of Works Cited

A list of works cited is an alphabetical list of the sources you have referred to in your essay. (If your instructor asks you to list everything

DIRECTORY TO MLA STYLE FOR WORKS-CITED ENTRIES

(Continued)

you have read as background, call the list *Works Consulted.*) Here are some guidelines for preparing such a list:

- Start your list on a separate page after the text of your essay and any notes.

- Continue the consecutive numbering of pages.

- Center the heading *Works Cited* an inch from the top of the page; do not underline or italicize it or enclose it in quotation marks. Double-space between the heading and the first entry, and double-space the entire list.
- Start each entry flush with the left margin, and indent subsequent lines one-half inch or five spaces.
- List your sources alphabetically by author's (or editor's) last name. If the author is unknown, alphabetize the source by the first word of the title, disregarding *A, An,* or *The.*

The sample works-cited entries that follow observe MLA's advice to underline words that are often italicized in print. If you wish to use italics instead, first check with your instructor.

Books

The basic format for a works-cited entry for a book is outlined on pp. 80–81. For an online book, see p. 97.

1. ONE AUTHOR

Winchester, Simon. <u>The Meaning of Everything: The Story of the
   Oxford English Dictionary</u>. New York: Oxford UP, 2003.

2. TWO OR THREE AUTHORS

Give the first author listed on the title page, last name first; then list the name(s) of the other author(s) in regular order, with a comma between authors and the word *and* before the last one.

Martineau, Jane, Desmond Shawe-Taylor, and Jonathon Bate.
   <u>Shakespeare in Art</u>. London: Merrill, 2003.

3. FOUR OR MORE AUTHORS

Give the first author listed on the title page, followed by a comma and *et al.* ("and others"), or list all the names, since the use of *et al.* diminishes the importance of the other contributors.

> Lupton, Ellen, Jennifer Tobias, Alicia Imperiale, Grace Jeffers, and
>> Randi Mates. <u>Skin: Surface, Substance, and Design</u>. New York:
>> Princeton Architectural, 2002.

4. ORGANIZATION AS AUTHOR

Give the name of the group listed on the title page as the author, even if the same group published the book.

> Getty Trust Publications. <u>Seeing the Getty Center/Seeing the Getty
>> Gardens</u>. Los Angeles: Getty Trust Publications, 2000.

5. UNKNOWN AUTHOR

Begin the entry with the title, and list the work alphabetically by the first word of the title after any initial *A, An,* or *The.*

> <u>New Concise World Atlas</u>. New York: Oxford UP, 2003.

6. TWO OR MORE BOOKS BY THE SAME AUTHOR(S)

Arrange the entries alphabetically by title. Include the name(s) of the author(s) in the first entry, but in subsequent entries, use three hyphens followed by a period.

> Lorde, Audre. <u>A Burst of Light</u>. Ithaca: Firebrand, 1988.

> ---. <u>Sister Outsider</u>. Trumansburg: Crossing, 1984.

If you cite a work by one author who is also listed as the first coauthor of another work you cite, list the single-author work first, and repeat the author's name in the entry for the coauthored work. Also repeat the author's name if you cite a work in which that author is listed as the first of a different set of coauthors. In other words, use three hyphens only when the work is by *exactly* the same author(s) as the previous entry.

7. EDITOR

Treat an editor as an author, but add a comma and *ed.* (or *eds.*).

Wall, Cheryl A., ed. Changing Our Own Words: Essays on Criticism,
     Theory, and Writing by Black Women. New Brunswick: Rutgers
     UP, 1989.

8. AUTHOR AND EDITOR

If you have cited the body of the text, begin with the author's name. Then list the editor(s), introduced by *Ed.* ("Edited by"), after the title.

James, Henry. Portrait of a Lady. Ed. Leon Edel. Boston: Houghton,
     1963.

If you have cited the editor's contribution, begin with the name(s) of the editor(s), followed by a comma and *ed.* (or *eds.*). Then list the author's name, introduced by *By,* after the title.

Edel, Leon, ed. Portrait of a Lady. By Henry James. Boston:
     Houghton, 1963.

9. WORK IN AN ANTHOLOGY OR CHAPTER IN A BOOK WITH AN EDITOR

List the author(s) of the selection or chapter; its title; the title of the book in which the selection or chapter appears; *Ed.* and the name(s) of the editor(s); the publication information; and the inclusive page numbers of the selection or chapter.

Komunyakaa, Yusef. "Facing It." The Seagull Reader. Ed. Joseph
     Kelly. New York: Norton, 2000. 126-27.

If the selection was originally published in a periodical and you are asked to supply information for this original source, use the following format. *Rpt.* is the abbreviation for *Reprinted.*

SOURCE MAP: Citing books using MLA Style

Take information from the book's title page and copyright page (on the reverse side of the title page), not from the book's cover or a library catalog.

(1) *Author.* List the last name first, followed by a comma, the first name, and the middle initial (if given). Omit titles such as *MD*, *PhD*, or *Sir*; include suffixes after the name and a comma (*O'Driscoll, Gerald P., Jr.*). End with a period.

(2) *Title.* Underline or (if your instructor permits) italicize the title and any subtitle; capitalize all major words. End with a period.

(3) *City of publication.* If more than one city is given, use the first one listed. For foreign cities that may be unfamiliar to your readers, add an abbreviation of the country or province (*Cork, Ire.*). Follow it with a colon.

(4) *Publisher.* Give a shortened version of the publisher's name (*Harper* for *HarperCollins Publishers; Harcourt* for *Harcourt Brace; Oxford UP* for *Oxford University Press*). Follow it with a comma.

(5) *Year of publication.* Consult the copyright page. If more than one copyright date is given, use the most recent one. End with a period.

For a book by one author, use the following format:

Last name, First name. Title of book. City: Publisher, Year.

A citation for the book on p. 81 would look like this:

AUTHOR, LAST NAME FIRST   TITLE AND SUBTITLE, UNDERLINED

Twitchell, James B. Living It Up: America's Love Affair with Luxury. New York:

Simon, 2002. ———— PUBLISHER'S CITY AND NAME, ————
                            YEAR OF PUBLICATION

———— DOUBLE-SPACE; INDENT ONE-HALF INCH OR FIVE SPACES

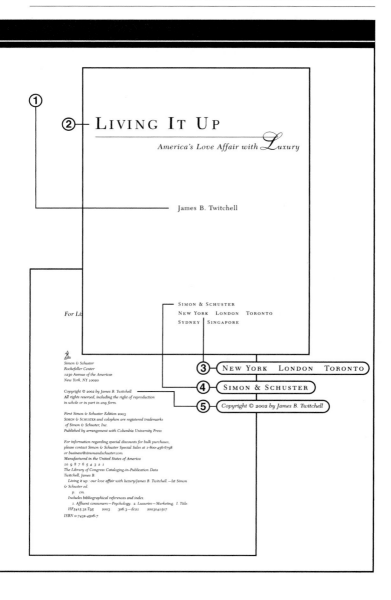

① ②— LIVING IT UP

America's Love Affair with Luxury

James B. Twitchell

For Li

Simon & Schuster
Rockefeller Center
1230 Avenue of the Americas
New York, NY 10020

SIMON & SCHUSTER
NEW YORK   LONDON   TORONTO
SYDNEY │ SINGAPORE

③—(NEW YORK   LONDON   TORONTO)

④—(SIMON & SCHUSTER)

Copyright © 2002 by James B. Twitchell
All rights reserved, including the right of reproduction
in whole or in part in any form.

⑤—(*Copyright © 2002 by James B. Twitchell*)

First Simon & Schuster Edition 2003
SIMON & SCHUSTER and colophon are registered trademarks
of Simon & Schuster, Inc.
Published by arrangement with Columbia University Press

For information regarding special discounts for bulk purchases,
please contact Simon & Schuster Special Sales at 1-800-456-6798
or business@simonandschuster.com.
Manufactured in the United States of America
10 9 8 7 6 5 4 3 2 1
The Library of Congress Cataloging-in-Publication Data
Twitchell, James B.
  Living it up : our love affair with luxury/James B. Twitchell. —1st Simon
& Schuster ed.
    p.   cm.
  Includes bibliographical references and index.
    1. Affluent consumers—Psychology   2. Luxuries—Marketing   I. Title
  HF5415.32.T95   2003   306.3—dc21   2003041507
ISBN 0-7432-4506-7

Byatt, A. S. "The Thing in the Forest." New Yorker 3 June 2002:
    80-89. Rpt. in The O. Henry Prize Stories 2003. Ed. Laura
    Furman. New York: Anchor, 2003. 3-22.

For inclusive page numbers up to 99, note all digits in the second
number. For numbers above 99, note only the last two digits and any
others that change in the second number (*115-18, 1378-79, 296-301*).

10. TWO OR MORE ITEMS FROM AN ANTHOLOGY

Include the anthology itself in your list of works cited. If the title
page uses the term *compiler(s)* rather than *editor(s),* use the abbreviation *comp.* (or *comps.*) instead of *ed.* (or *eds.*).

Walker, Dale L., ed. Westward: A Fictional History of the American
    West. New York: Forge, 2003.

Also list each selection separately by its author and title, followed
by a cross-reference to the anthology. Alphabetize all entries.

Estleman, Loren D. "Big Tim Magoon and the Wild West." Walker
    391-404.

Salzer, Susan K. "Miss Libbie Tells All." Walker 199-212.

11. TRANSLATION

Begin the entry with the author's name, and give the translator's
name, preceded by *Trans.* ("Translated by"), after the title.

Hietamies, Laila. Red Moon over White Sea. Trans. Borje Vahamaki.
    Beaverton, OR: Aspasia, 2000.

If you cite a translated selection from an anthology, add *Trans.*
and the translator's name before the title of the anthology.

Horace. The Art of Poetry. Trans. Smith Palmer Bovie. The Critical
Tradition: Classic Texts and Contemporary Trends. Ed. David H.
Richter. 2nd ed. Boston: Bedford, 1998. 68-78.

12. BOOK IN A LANGUAGE OTHER THAN ENGLISH

If necessary, you may provide a translation of the book's title in
brackets. You may also choose to give the English name of a foreign
city in brackets.

Benedetti, Mario. La borra del café [The Coffee Grind]. Buenos Aires:
Sudamericana, 2000.

13. EDITION OTHER THAN THE FIRST

Add the information, in abbreviated form, after the title.

Walker, John A. Art in the Age of Mass Media. 3rd ed. London: Pluto,
2001.

14. MULTIVOLUME WORK

If you cite only one volume, give the volume number after the title,
using the abbreviation *Vol.* You may give the number of volumes in the
complete work at the end of the entry, using the abbreviation *vols.*

Ch'oe, Yong-Ho, Peter Lee, and William Theodore De Barry, eds.
Sources of Korean Tradition. Vol. 2. New York: Columbia UP,
2000. 2 vols.

If you cite two or more volumes, give the number of volumes in
the complete work after the title.

Ch'oe, Yong-Ho, Peter Lee, and William Theodore De Barry, eds. Sources
of Korean Tradition. 2 vols. New York: Columbia UP, 2000.

15. PREFACE, FOREWORD, INTRODUCTION, OR AFTERWORD

Begin with the author of the item and the item title (not underlined, italicized, or in quotation marks). Then give the title of the book and the book's author (preceded by the word *By*) or editor (preceded by *Ed.*). If the same person wrote or edited both the book and the cited item, use just the last name after *By* or *Ed.* List the page numbers of the item at the end of the entry.

Atwan, Robert. Foreword. The Best American Essays 2002.

Ed. Stephen Jay Gould. Boston: Houghton, 2002.

viii-xii.

16. ENTRY IN A REFERENCE WORK

List the author of the entry, if known. If no author is identified, begin with the title. For a well-known reference work, just note the edition number and year of publication or designate the edition by its year of publication. If the entries in the work are in alphabetical order, you need not give volume or page numbers. (For an electronic version of a reference work, see p. 99.)

"Hero." Merriam-Webster's Collegiate Dictionary. 11th ed.

2003.

Kettering, Alison McNeil. "Art Nouveau." World Book Encyclopedia.

2002 ed.

17. BOOK THAT IS PART OF A SERIES

Cite the series name as it appears on the title page, followed by any series number.

Nichanian, Marc, and Vartan Matiossian, eds. Yeghishe Charents:

Poet of the Revolution. Armenian Studies Ser. 5. Costa Mesa:

Mazda, 2003.

18. REPUBLICATION

To cite a modern edition of an older book, add the original publication date, followed by a period, after the title.

Scott, Walter. <u>Kenilworth</u>. 1821. New York: Dodd, 1956.

19. PUBLISHER'S IMPRINT

If a book is published under a publisher's imprint (indicated on the title page), hyphenate the imprint and the publisher's name.

Gilligan, Carol. <u>The Birth of Pleasure: A New Map of Love</u>. New York: Vintage-Random, 2003.

20. BOOK WITH A TITLE WITHIN THE TITLE

Do not underline or italicize the title of a book within the title of a book you are citing. Enclose in quotation marks the title of a short work within a book title, and underline or italicize it as you do the rest of the title.

Mullaney, Julie. <u>Arundhati Roy's</u> The God of Small Things: <u>A Reader's Guide</u>. New York: Continuum, 2002.

Rhynes, Martha. <u>"I, Too, Sing America": The Story of Langston Hughes</u>. Greensboro: Morgan, 2002.

21. SACRED TEXT

To cite individual published editions of sacred books, begin with the title. If a specified version is not part of the title, list the version after the title. If you are not citing a particular edition, do not include sacred texts in the works-cited list.

Periodicals

The basic format for a works-cited entry for a periodical article appears on pp. 86–87.

SOURCE MAP: Citing articles from periodicals using MLA Style

(1) *Author.* List the last name first, followed by a comma, the first name, and the middle initial (if given). Omit titles such as *MD*, *PhD*, or *Sir;* include suffixes after the name and a comma (*O'Driscoll, Gerald P., Jr.*). End with a period.

(2) *Article title.* Enclose the title and any subtitle in quotation marks, and capitalize all major words. The closing period goes inside the closing quotation mark.

(3) *Periodical title.* Underline or italicize the periodical title (excluding any initial *A*, *An*, or *The*), and capitalize all major words. For journals, give the volume number; if each issue starts with page 1, include the issue number as well.

(4) *Date of publication.* For journals, list the year in parentheses, followed by a colon. For monthly magazines, list the month and year. For weekly magazines and newspapers, list the day, month, and year.

(5) *Inclusive page numbers.* For page numbers up to 99, note all digits in the second number. For numbers above 99, note only the last two digits and any others that change in the second number (*115-18, 1378-79, 296-301*). Include section letters for newspapers. End with a period.

For a journal article, use the following format:

Last name, First name. "Title of article." Journal Volume number (year): Page number(s).

For a newspaper article, use the following format:

Last name, First name. "Title." Newspaper Date, Edition (if any): Section number (if any): Page number(s) (including section letter, if any).

For a magazine article, use the following format:

Last name, First name. "Title of article." Magazine Date: Page number(s).

A citation for the magazine article on p. 317 would look like this:

AUTHOR, LAST NAME FIRST   ARTICLE TITLE AND SUBTITLE, IN QUOTATION MARKS

Conniff, Richard. "Counting Carbons: How Much Greenhouse Gas Does Your Family

Produce?" Discover Aug. 2005: 54-61.   DOUBLE-SPACE

PERIODICAL TITLE   DATE   INCLUSIVE PAGE NUMBERS
UNDERLINED

INDENT ONE-HALF INCH OR FIVE SPACES

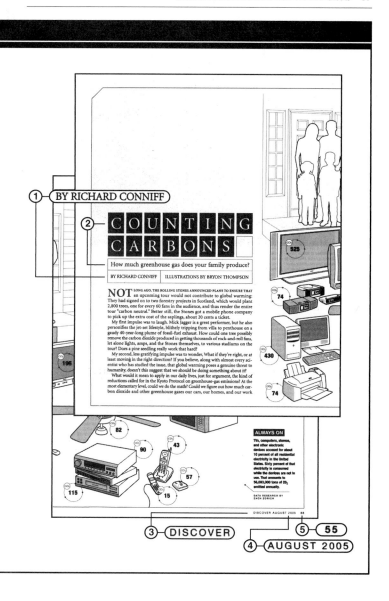

① BY RICHARD CONNIFF

② C O U N T I N G
C A R B O N S

How much greenhouse gas does your family produce?

BY RICHARD CONNIFF | ILLUSTRATIONS BY BRYON THOMPSON

NOT LONG AGO, THE ROLLING STONES ANNOUNCED PLANS TO ENSURE THAT an upcoming tour would not contribute to global warming: They had signed on to two forestry projects in Scotland, which would plant 2,800 trees, one for every 60 fans in the audience, and thus render the entire tour "carbon neutral." Better still, the Stones got a mobile phone company to pick up the extra cost of the saplings, about 20 cents a ticket.

My first impulse was to laugh. Mick Jagger is a great performer, but he also personifies the jet-set lifestyle, blithely tripping from villa to penthouse on a gaudy 40-year-long plume of fossil-fuel exhaust. How could one tree possibly remove the carbon dioxide produced in getting thousands of rock-and-roll fans, let alone lights, amps, and the Stones themselves, to various stadiums on the tour? Does a pine seedling really work that hard?

My second, less gratifying impulse was to wonder. What if they're right, or at least moving in the right direction? If you believe, along with almost every scientist who has studied the issue, that global warming poses a genuine threat to humanity, doesn't this suggest that we should be doing something about it?

What would it mean to apply in our daily lives, just for argument, the kind of reductions called for in the Kyoto Protocol on greenhouse-gas emissions? At the most elementary level, could we do the math? Could we figure out how much carbon dioxide and other greenhouse gases our cars, our homes, and our work

ALWAYS ON

TVs, computers, stereos, and other electronic devices account for about 10 percent of all residential electricity in the United States. Sixty percent of that electricity is consumed while the devices are not in use. That amounts to 56,093,000 tons of CO₂ emitted annually.

DATA RESEARCH BY ZACH ZORICH

DISCOVER AUGUST 2005 88

③ DISCOVER

④ AUGUST 2005

⑤ 55

22. ARTICLE IN A JOURNAL PAGINATED BY VOLUME

Follow the journal title with the volume number in arabic numerals.

Gigante, Denise. "The Monster in the Rainbow: Keats and the
Science of Life." PMLA 117 (2002): 433-48.

23. ARTICLE IN A JOURNAL PAGINATED BY ISSUE

If each issue begins with page 1, put a period and the issue number after the volume number.

Zivley, Sherry Lutz. "Sylvia Plath's Transformations of Modernist
Paintings." College Literature 29.3 (2002): 35-56.

24. ARTICLE THAT SKIPS PAGES

When an article skips pages, give only the first page number and a plus sign.

Tyrnauer, Matthew. "Empire by Martha." Vanity Fair Sept. 2002:
364+.

25. ARTICLE WITH A TITLE WITHIN THE TITLE

Enclose in single quotation marks the title of a short work within an article title. Underline or italicize the title of a book within an article title.

Frey, Leonard H. "Irony and Point of View in 'That Evening Sun.'"
Faulkner Studies 2 (1953): 33-40.

26. ARTICLE IN A MONTHLY MAGAZINE

Put the month (or months, hyphenated) before the year. Abbreviate months other than *May, June,* and *July.* Do not include volume or issue numbers.

Fonda, Daren. "Saving the Dead." Life Apr. 2000: 69-72.

27. ARTICLE IN A WEEKLY MAGAZINE

Include the day, month, and year in that order, with no commas between them. Do not include volume or issue numbers.

Gilgoff, Dan. "Unusual Suspects." US News and World Report 26 Nov. 2001: 51.

28. ARTICLE IN A NEWSPAPER

After the author and title of the article, give the name of the newspaper as it appears on the front page but without any initial *A, An,* or *The.* For locally published newspapers, add the city in brackets after the name if it is not part of the name. Then give the date and the edition (if listed), followed by a colon, a space, the section number or letter (if listed), and the page number(s). If the article does not appear on consecutive pages, give the first page followed by a plus sign.

Bernstein, Nina. "On Lucille Avenue, the Immigration Debate." New York Times 26 June 2006, late ed.: A1+.

29. ARTICLE IN A COLLECTION OF REPRINTED ARTICLES

First give the citation for the original publication. Then give the citation for the collection in which the article is reprinted. Insert *Rpt. in* ("Reprinted in") between the two citations. Use *Comp.* to identify the compiler. *Ed.* and *Trans.* are other common abbreviations used in citing a collection.

Quindlen, Anna. "Playing God on No Sleep." Newsweek 2 July 2001: 64. Rpt. in The Best American Magazine Writing 2002. Comp. Amer. Soc. of Magazine Eds. New York: Perennial, 2002. 458-62.

30. EDITORIAL OR LETTER TO THE EDITOR

Use the label *Editorial* or *Letter,* not underlined, italicized, or in quotation marks, after the title or, if there is no title, after the author's name, if given.

Magee, Doug. "Soldier's Home." Editorial. Nation 26 Mar. 1988: 400-01.

31. REVIEW

List the reviewer's name and the title of the review, if any, followed by *Rev. of* and the title and author, director, or other creator of the work reviewed. Then add the publication information.

Franklin, Nancy. "Dead On." Rev. of Deadwood, by David Milch.

New Yorker 12 June 2006: 158-59.

32. UNSIGNED ARTICLE

Begin with the article title, alphabetizing the entry according to the first word after any initial *A, An,* or *The.*

"Performance of the Week." Time 6 Oct. 2003: 18.

Electronic Sources

Electronic sources such as Web sites differ from print sources in the ease with which they can be — and frequently are — changed, updated, or even eliminated. In addition, the various electronic media do not organize their works the same way. For these reasons, as the *MLA Handbook for Writers of Research Papers* notes, "References to electronic works . . . must provide more information than print citations generally offer."

The most commonly cited electronic sources are documents from Web sites and databases. The entry for such a source may include up to five basic elements, as in the following list, but must always include the last two:

- *Author.* List the last name first, followed by a comma and the first name, and end with a period. If no author is given, begin the entry with the title.

- *Title.* Enclose the title and subtitle of the document in quotation marks unless you are citing an entire site or an online book, both of which should be underlined or italicized. Capitalize all major words, and end with a period inside the closing quotation marks.

- *Print publication information.* Give any information the document provides about a previous or simultaneous publication in print, using the guidelines in the previous sections.

- *Electronic publication information.* List all of the following items that you can find, with a period after each one: the title of the site, underlined or italicized, with all major words capitalized; the editor(s) of the site, preceded by *Ed.*; the version number of the site, preceded by *Vers.*; the date of electronic publication or of the latest update, with the month, if any, abbreviated except for *May, June,* and *July*; and the name of any sponsoring institution or organization. (The sponsor's name usually appears at the bottom of the site's home page.)

- *Access information.* Give the most recent date you accessed the source, abbreviating months as noted above; the URL enclosed in angle brackets; and a period after the closing bracket. In general, give the complete URL, including the opening http, ftp, gopher, telnet, or news. If the URL is very long and complicated, however, substitute the URL of the site's search page instead. If the site does not provide a usable URL for individual documents and citing the search page is inappropriate, give the URL of the site's home page. To help readers find the document through links on the home page, do the following: after the URL of the home page, give the word Path and a colon, and then list the sequence of links. Use semicolons between the links and a period at the end. Whenever a URL will not fit on one line, break it only after a slash; do not add a hyphen at the break.

Further guidelines for citing electronic sources can be found in the *MLA Handbook for Writers of Research Papers* and online at www.mla.org.

33. ARTICLE FROM AN ONLINE DATABASE OR A SUBSCRIPTION SERVICE

The basic format for citing a work from a database appears on pp. 94–95.

For a work from an online database, provide all of following elements that are available: the author's name (if given); the title of the work in quotation marks; any print publication information; the name of the online database, underlined or italicized; the name of its editor (if any), preceded by *Ed.*; the date of the most recent revision; and the name of any organization or institution with which the database is affiliated. End with the date of access and the URL, in angle brackets.

"Bolivia: Elecciones Presidenciales de 2002." Political Database of

the Americas. 1999. Georgetown U and Organization of Amer.

States. 12 Nov. 2003 <http://www.georgetown.edu/pdba/

Elecdata/Bolivia/pres02B.html>.

For a work from a library subscription service, after the information about the work give the name of the database, underlined or italicized, if you know it; the name of the service; the library; the date of access; and the URL of the service's home page, if you know it.

Gordon, Andrew. "It's Not Such a Wonderful Life: The Neurotic

George Bailey." American Journal of Psychoanalysis 54.3

(1994): 219-33. PsycINFO. EBSCOhost. City U of New York,

Graduate Center Lib. 26 Oct. 2003 <http://www.epnet.com>.

For a work from a personal online subscription service such as America Online, follow the guidelines in this chapter for the appropriate type of work. End the entry with the URL of the specific work or, if it is long and complicated, the URL of the service's search page. If, however, the service supplies no URL or one that is not accessible to others, you need to provide other access information at the end of the entry. Depending on the service's retrieval system, give either the word Keyword followed by a colon and the keyword you used or the word Path followed by a colon and the sequence of links you followed, separated with semicolons.

> "Steps in Reading a Poem." AOL's Academic Assistance Center. 11
>   Feb. 2004. Path: Reading & Learning; Poetry; Analysis and
>   Interpreting Poetry.

> Weeks, W. William. "Beyond the Ark." Nature Conservancy Mar.-Apr.
>   1999. America Online. 2 Apr. 1999. Keyword: Ecology.

34. WORK FROM A WEB SITE

For basic information on citing a work from a Web site, see pp. 100–101. Include all of the following elements that are available: the author; the title of the document; the name of the Web site, underlined or italicized; the name of the editor, if any; the date of publication or the latest update; the name of the institution or organization associated with the site; the date of access; and the document's URL.

> "Hands Off Public Broadcasting." Media Matters for America.
>   24 May 2005. Media Matters for America. 31 May 2005
>   <http://www.mediamatters.org/items/200505240001>.

> Stauder, Ellen Keck. "Darkness Audible: Negative Capability and Mark
>   Doty's 'Nocturne in Black and Gold.'" Romantic Circles Praxis
>   Series. Ed. Orrin Wang. 2003. 28 Sept. 2003 <http://
>   www.rc.umd.edu/praxis/poetics/stauder/stauder.html>.

For a personal Web site, include the name of the person who created the site; the title, underlined or italicized, or (if there is no title) a description such as *Home page*; the date of the last update, if given; the access information; and the URL.

SOURCE MAP: Citing articles from databases using MLA Style

Libraries pay for services—such as InfoTrac, EBSCOhost, ProQuest, and LexisNexis—that provide access to huge databases of electronic articles.

(1) *Author.* List the last name first.

(2) *Article title.* Enclose the title and any subtitle in quotation marks.

(3) *Periodical title.* Underline or italicize it. Exclude any initial *A, An,* or *The.*

(4) *Volume number.* Also list the issue number if appropriate.

(5) *Date of publication.* Give the year for journals; the month and year for monthly magazines; the day, month, and year for weekly magazines and newspapers.

(6) *Inclusive page number(s).* Include section letters for newspapers, if relevant. If only the first page number is given, follow it with a hyphen, a space, and a period.

(7) *Name of the database.* Underline or italicize the name.

(8) *Name of the subscription service, if available.* Here, it is InfoTrac.

(9) *Name of the library where you accessed the article.* Also list the city and, if necessary, an abbreviation for the state (*Burnt Hills, NY*).

(10) End with the date you accessed the article and a brief URL for the database.

For an article from a database, use the following format:

[Citation format for journal, magazine, or newspaper article — see pp. 85–90].
     Name of database. Name of service. Library name, Location. Date accessed
     <Brief Web address>.

A citation for the article on p. 95 would look like this:

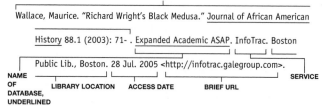

CITATION INFORMATION FOR THE ARTICLE

Wallace, Maurice. "Richard Wright's Black Medusa." Journal of African American

     History 88.1 (2003): 71- . Expanded Academic ASAP. InfoTrac. Boston

     Public Lib., Boston. 28 Jul. 2005 <http://infotrac.galegroup.com>.

NAME OF DATABASE, UNDERLINED   LIBRARY LOCATION   ACCESS DATE   BRIEF URL   SERVICE

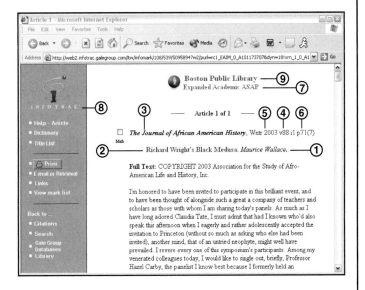

Lunsford, Andrea A. Home page. 27 Mar. 2003. 17 May 2006
>   <http://www.stanford.edu/~lunsfor1/>.

35. ENTIRE WEB SITE

Follow the guidelines for a specific work from the Web, but begin with the title of the entire site and the names of the editor(s), if any.

Electronic Poetry Center. Ed. Charles Bernstein, Kenneth
>   Goldsmith, Martin Spinelli, and Patrick Durgin. 2003. Poetics
>   Program/Dept. of Media Study, SUNY Buffalo. 26 Sept. 2003
>   <http://wings.buffalo.edu/epc/>.

Weather.com. 2006. Weather Channel Interactive. 13 Mar. 2006
>   <http://www.weather.com>.

36. ACADEMIC COURSE OR DEPARTMENT WEB SITE

For a course site, include the name of the instructor, the title of the course, a description such as *Course home page,* the dates of the course, the department name, the institution, and the access information.

Lunsford, Andrea A. Memory and Media. Course home
>   page. Sept.-Dec. 2002. Dept. of English, Stanford U.
>   13 Mar. 2003 <http://www.stanford.edu/class/
>   english12sc>.

For a department site, give the department name, a description such as *Dept. home page,* the institution, and the access information.

English. Dept. home page. Amherst Coll. 5 Apr. 2006
>   <http://www.amherst.edu/~english/>.

37. WEB LOG (BLOG)

For an entire Web log, give the author's name; the title of the Web log; the description *Web log*; the date of the most recent update; the sponsor of the site, if any; the date of access; and the URL. (Because the MLA currently provides no guidelines for documenting a blog, these models are based on MLA guidelines for Web sites and short works from Web sites.)

> Atrios. Eschaton. Web log. 27 June 2006. 27 June 2006
> <http://www.atrios.blogspot.com/>.

For a post or comment on a Web log, give the author's name; the title of the post or comment, if any; the description *Web log post* or *Web log comment*; and the publication and access information.

> Parker, Randall. "Growth Rate for Electric Hybrid Vehicle
> Market Debated." Web log post. FuturePundit. 20 May
> 2005. 24 May 2005 <http://www.futurepundit.com/
> archives/002783.html>.

38. ONLINE BOOK

Cite an online book as you would a print book (see models 1–21). After the print publication information (city, publisher, and year), if any, give the electronic publication information, the date of access, and the URL.

> Euripides. The Trojan Women. Trans. Gilbert Murray. New York:
> Oxford UP, 1915. 12 Oct. 2003 <http://www.sacred-texts.com/
> cla/eurip/trojan.htm>.

Cite a part of an online book as you would a part of a print book (see models 9 and 15). Give the available print and electronic publication information, the date of access, and the URL of the part.

Riis, Jacob. "The Genesis of the Gang." The Battle with the Slum.
New York: Macmillan, 1902. Bartleby.com: Great Books Online.
2000. 31 Mar. 2005 <http://www.bartleby.com/175/9.html>.

39. ONLINE POEM

Include the poet's name and the title of the poem, followed by
the print publication information for the poem (if applicable). End
with electronic publication information, the date of access, and the
URL.

Dickinson, Emily. "The Grass." Poems: Emily Dickinson. Boston,
1891. Humanities Text Initiative American Verse Project.
Ed. Nancy Kushigian. 1995. U of Michigan. 6 Jan 2006
<http://www.hti.umich.edu>.

40. ARTICLE IN AN ONLINE JOURNAL, MAGAZINE, OR NEWSPAPER

Cite the article as you would an article from a print journal, magazine, or newspaper (see models 22–28). End with the total number
of pages, paragraphs, parts, or other sections, if numbered; the date of
access; and the URL.

Burt, Stephen. "The True Legacy of Marianne Moore, Modernist
Monument." Slate 11 Nov. 2003. 12 Nov. 2003 <http://
slate.msn.com/id/2091081/>.

Gallagher, Brian. "Greta Garbo Is Sad: Some Historical Reflections
on the Paradoxes of Stardom in the American Film Industry,
1910-1960." Images: A Journal of Film and Popular Culture 3
(1997): 7 pts. 7 Aug. 2002 <http://imagesjournal.com/
issue03/infocus.htm>.

Shea, Christopher. "Five Truths about Tuition." New York Times
    Online 9 Nov. 2003. 11 Nov. 2003 <http://www.nytimes.com/
    2003/11/09/edlife/1109SHT.html>.

41. ONLINE EDITORIAL OR LETTER TO THE EDITOR

Include the word *Editorial* or *Letter* after the author (if given) and
title (if any). End with the name of the Web site, the date of electronic
publication, the date of access, and the URL.

"The Funding Gap." Editorial. Washingtonpost.com 5 Nov. 2003. 9
    Nov. 2003 <http://www.washingtonpost.com/wp-dyn/articles/
    A1087-2003Nov5.html>.

Piccato, Pablo. Letter. New York Times Online 9 Nov. 2003.
    9 Nov. 2003 <http://www.nytimes.com/2003/11/09/opinion/
    L09IMMI.html>.

42. ONLINE REVIEW

Cite an online review as you would a print review (see model 31).
End with the name of the Web site, the date of electronic publication,
the date of access, and the URL.

O'Hehir, Andrew. "The Nightmare in Iraq." Rev. of Gunner Palace, dir.
    Michael Tucker and Petra Epperlein. Salon 4 Mar. 2005. 24 May
    2005 <http://www.salon.com/ent/movies/review/2005/03/04/
    gunner/index.html>.

43. ENTRY IN AN ONLINE REFERENCE WORK

Cite the entry as you would an entry from a print reference work
(see model 16). End with the sponsor and access information.

SOURCE MAP: Citing works from Web sites using MLA Style

You may need to browse other parts of a site to find some elements, and some sites may omit elements. Uncover as much information as you can.

(1) *Author of the work.* List the last name first, followed by a comma, the first name, and the middle initial (if given). End with a period. If no author is given, begin with the title.

(2) *Title of the work.* Enclose the title and any subtitle of the work in quotation marks.

(3) *Title of the Web site.* Give the title of the entire Web site, underlined or italicized. Where there is no clear title, use *Home page* without underlining or italicizing it.

(4) *Date of publication or latest update.* Give the most recent date.

(5) *Name of the sponsoring organization.* The sponsor's name often appears at the bottom of the site's home page.

(6) *Access information.* Give the most recent date you accessed the work. Give the complete URL, enclosed in angle brackets. If the URL is very long and complicated, give the URL of the site's search page instead. If the URL will not fit on one line, break it only after a slash, and do not add a hyphen.

For a work from a Web site, use the following format:

Last name, First name. "Title of work." Title of Web site. Date of publication or latest update. Sponsoring organization. Date accessed <Web address>.

A citation for the work on p. 101 would look like this:

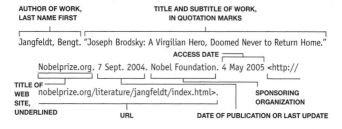

AUTHOR OF WORK,
LAST NAME FIRST

TITLE AND SUBTITLE OF WORK,
IN QUOTATION MARKS

Jangfeldt, Bengt. "Joseph Brodsky: A Virgilian Hero, Doomed Never to Return Home."

ACCESS DATE

Nobelprize.org. 7 Sept. 2004. Nobel Foundation. 4 May 2005 <http://

TITLE OF
WEB   nobelprize.org/literature/jangfeldt/index.html>.   SPONSORING
SITE,   ORGANIZATION
UNDERLINED   URL   DATE OF PUBLICATION OR LAST UPDATE

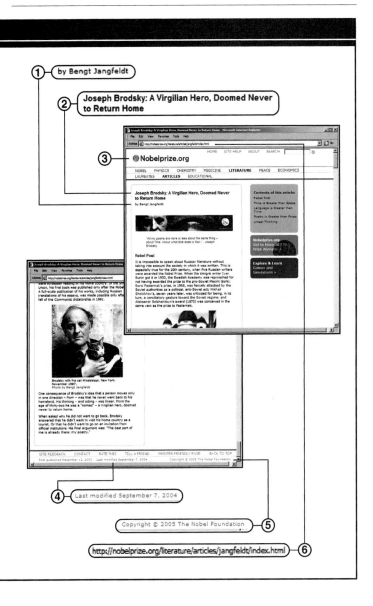

① by Bengt Jangfeldt

② Joseph Brodsky: A Virgilian Hero, Doomed Never to Return Home

③ @Nobelprize.org

④ Last modified September 7, 2004

⑤ Copyright © 2005 The Nobel Foundation

⑥ http://nobelprize.org/literature/articles/jangfeldt/index.html

"Tour de France." <u>Encyclopaedia Britannica Online</u>. 2006. Encyclo-
paedia Britannica. 21 May 2006 <http://www.britannica.com>.

44. ENTRY IN A WIKI

Because wiki content is collectively edited, do not include an
author. Include the title of the entry; the name of the wiki; the date of
the latest update; the sponsor of the wiki, if any; access information;
and the URL. Check with your instructor before using a wiki as a source.
(The MLA does not provide guidelines on citing wikis; this model is
based on the MLA's guidelines on citing short works from Web sites.)

"Fédération Internationale de Football Association." <u>Wikipedia</u>.
27 June 2006. Wikimedia Foundation. 27 June 2006 <http://
en.wikipedia.org/wiki/FIFA>.

45. POSTING TO A DISCUSSION GROUP

Begin with the author's name; the title of the posting, in quotation marks; the description *Online posting*, not underlined or italicized
or in quotation marks; and the date of posting. For a listserv posting,
then give the name of the listserv; the date of access; and the URL of
the listserv, the email address of its moderator, or (preferably) the URL
of an archival version of the posting.

Daly, Catherine. "Poetry Slams." Online posting. 29 Aug. 2003.
SUNY Buffalo Poetics Discussion List. 1 Oct. 2003 <http://
listserv.acsu.buffalo.edu/archives/poetics.html>.

For a newsgroup posting, end with the date of access and the name of
the newsgroup in angle brackets, with the prefix *news*.

Stonehouse, Robert. "Repeated Words in Shakespeare's Sonnets."
Online posting. 27 July 2003. 24 Sept. 2003 <news:humanities
.lit.authors.shakespeare>.

46. EMAIL

Include the writer's name; the subject line, in quotation marks; a description of the message that mentions the recipient; and the date of the message. (MLA style hyphenates *e-mail*.)

Harris, Jay. "Thoughts on Impromptu Stage Productions." E-mail to
    the author. 16 July 2006.

47. REAL-TIME COMMUNICATION

In citing a posting in a real-time forum, include all of the following information that is available: the name(s) of any speaker(s) you are citing; a description of the event; its date; the name of the forum; the access date; and the URL. Always cite an archival version of the posting if one is available.

Hong, Billy. Billy's Final Draft: Homeless Essay. 14 Oct. 2003.
    LinguaMOO. 12 Nov. 2003 <http://lingua.utdallas.edu:7000/
    25871/>.

48. COMPUTER SOFTWARE OR VIDEO GAME

Include the title, underlined or italicized, version number (if given), and publication information. If you are citing downloaded software, replace the publication information with the date of access and the URL.

The Sims 2. Redwood City: Electronic Arts, 2004.

Web Cache Illuminator. Vers. 4.02. 12 Nov. 2003 <http://www.tucows
    .com/adnload/332309_126245.html>.

49. PERIODICALLY REVISED CD-ROM

For a periodically revised CD-ROM, begin with the author, title, and any available print publication information. Then give the term

CD-ROM, the name of the company or group producing it, and the electronic publication date (month and year, if available).

> Ashenfelter, Orley, and Kathryn Graddy. "Auctions and the Price
>
> of Art." Journal of Economic Literature 41.3 (2003): 763-87.
>
> CD-ROM. Amer. Economic Assn. Sept. 2003.

50. SINGLE-ISSUE CD-ROM

Cite a CD-ROM like a book if it is not regularly updated. Add the term *CD-ROM* and, if appropriate, the number of the electronic edition, release, or version. If you are citing only a part of the source, indicate which part and end with the numbers of the part, if provided.

> Cambridge Advanced Learner's Dictionary. CD-ROM. Cambridge:
>
> Cambridge UP, 2003.

51. MULTIDISC CD-ROM

If the CD-ROM includes more than one disc, include the term *CD-ROM* and either the total number of discs (*3 discs*) or, if you used material from only one, the number of that disc.

> IRIS: Immigration Research Information Service, LawDesk. CD-ROM.
>
> Disc 2. Eagon, MN: West, 2003.

Other Sources (Including Online Versions)

If an online version is not shown here, use the appropriate model for the source and then end with the date of access and the URL.

52. REPORT OR PAMPHLET

Cite a report or pamphlet by following the guidelines for a print or an online book.

Allen, Katherine, and Lee Rainie. Parents Online. Washington:
    Pew Internet and Amer. Life Project, 2002.

Environmental Working Group. Dead in the Water. 2006.
    Environmental Working Group. 24 Apr. 2006
    <http://www.ewg.org/reports/deadzone/>.

53. GOVERNMENT PUBLICATION

Begin with the author, if identified. Otherwise, start with the
name of the government, followed by the agency and any subdivision.
Use abbreviations if they can be readily understood. Then give the
title. For congressional documents, cite the number, session, and
house of Congress (using *S* for Senate and *H* or *HR* for House of Representatives); the type (*Report, Resolution, Document*) in abbreviated
form; and the number of the material. If you cite the *Congressional
Record,* give only the date and page number(s). Otherwise, end with
the publication information. For print versions, the publisher is often
the Government Printing Office (GPO). For online versions, include
as much publication information as you can find and end with the
date of access and the URL.

Gregg, Judd. Report to Accompany the Genetic Information Act of
    2003. US 108th Cong., 1st sess. S. Rept. 108-22. Washington:
    GPO, 2003.

Kinsella, Kevin, and Victoria Velkoff. An Aging World: 2001. US
    Bureau of the Census. Washington: GPO, 2001.

United States. Environmental Protection Agency. Office of
    Emergency and Remedial Response. This Is Superfund. Jan.
    2000. 16 Aug. 2002 <http://www.epa.gov/superfund/
    students/clas_act/haz-ed/thisissf.htm>.

54. PUBLISHED PROCEEDINGS OF A CONFERENCE

Cite proceedings as you would a book. If the title doesn't include enough information about the conference, add necessary information after the title.

Cleary, John, and Gary Gurtler, eds. Proceedings of the Boston
Area Colloquium in Ancient Philosophy 2002. Boston: Brill
Academic, 2003.

55. UNPUBLISHED DISSERTATION OR THESIS

Enclose the title in quotation marks. Add the label *Diss.*, the school, and the year the work was accepted. If you are citing a thesis, use a label such as *MA thesis* (or whatever is appropriate) instead of *Diss.*

LeCourt, Donna. "The Self in Motion: The Status of the (Student)
Subject in Composition Studies." Diss. Ohio State U, 1993.

56. PUBLISHED DISSERTATION

Cite a published dissertation as a book, adding the identification *Diss.* and the university. If the dissertation was published by University Microfilms International, end the entry with *Ann Arbor: UMI,* the year, and the UMI number.

Yau, Rittchell Ann. The Portrayal of Immigration in a Selection of
Picture Books Published since 1970. Diss. U of San Francisco,
2003. Ann Arbor: UMI, 2003. 3103491.

57. DISSERTATION ABSTRACT

To cite the abstract of a dissertation using *Dissertation Abstracts International (DAI)*, include the *DAI* volume, year (in parentheses), and page number.

Huang-Tiller, Gillian C. "The Power of the Meta-Genre: Cultural,

Sexual, and Racial Politics of the American Modernist Sonnet."

Diss. U of Notre Dame, 2000. <u>DAI</u> 61 (2000): 1401.

58. UNPUBLISHED OR PERSONAL INTERVIEW

List the person interviewed, and then use the label *Telephone interview, Personal interview,* or *E-mail interview.* End with the date(s) the interview took place.

Freedman, Sasha. Personal interview. 10 Nov. 2006.

59. PUBLISHED OR BROADCAST INTERVIEW

List the person interviewed and then the title of the interview. If the interview has no title, use the label *Interview* and name the interviewer, if relevant. Then identify the source.

Ebert, Robert. Interview with Matthew Rothschild. <u>Progressive.</u>

Aug. 2003. 5 Oct. 2003 <http://www.progressive.org/aug03/

intv803.html>.

Taylor, Max. "Max Taylor on Winning." <u>Time</u> 13 Nov. 2000: 66.

To cite a broadcast interview, end with information about the program and the date(s) the interview took place.

Revkin, Andrew. Interview. <u>Fresh Air.</u> Natl. Public Radio. WNYC,

New York. 14 June 2006.

60. UNPUBLISHED LETTER

Cite a published letter as a work in an anthology (see model 9). If the letter is unpublished, follow this form:

Anzaldúa, Gloria. Letter to the author. 10 Sept. 2002.

61. MANUSCRIPT OR OTHER UNPUBLISHED WORK

Begin with the author's name and the title or, if there is no title, a description of the material. Then note the form of the material (such as *ms.* for *manuscript* or *ts.* for *typescript*) and any identifying numbers assigned to it. End by giving the name and location of the library or research institution housing the material, if applicable.

> Woolf, Virginia. "The Searchlight." Ts. Ser. III, Box 4, Item
>
> 184. Papers of Virginia Woolf, 1902-1956. Smith Coll.,
>
> Northampton.

62. LEGAL SOURCE

To cite a legal case, give the name of the case, the number of the case (using the abbreviation *No.*), the name of the court, and the date of the decision.

> Eldred v. Ashcroft. No. 01-618. Supreme Ct. of the US. 15 Jan. 2003.

To cite an act, give the name of the act followed by its Public Law (*Pub. L.*) number, the date the act was enacted, and its Statutes at Large (*Stat.*) cataloging number.

> Museum and Library Services Act of 2003. Pub. L. 108-81. 25 Sept.
>
> 2003. Stat. 117.991.

63. FILM, VIDEO, OR DVD

If you cite a particular person's work, start the entry with that person's name. In general, start with the title, underlined or italicized; then name the director, the distributor, and the year of release. Other contributors, such as writers or performers, may follow the director. If you cite a video or DVD instead of a theatrical release, include the original film release date (if relevant) and the label *Videocassette* or *DVD*.

Moore, Michael, dir. <u>Bowling for Columbine</u>. 2002.
        BowlingforColumbine.com. 30 Sept. 2005
        <http://www.bowlingforcolumbine.com/media/clips/index.php>.

<u>Spirited Away</u>. Dir. Hiyao Miyazaki. Perf. Daveigh Chase, Suzanne
        Pleshette, and Jason Marsden. 2001. DVD. Walt Disney Video,
        2003.

<u>Water</u>. Dir. Deepa Mehta. Fox Searchlight, 2006.

64. TELEVISION OR RADIO PROGRAM

In general, begin with the title of the program, underlined or italicized. Then list any important contributors (narrator, writer, director,
actors); the network; the local station and city, if any; and the broadcast date. To cite a particular person's work, begin the entry with that
name. To cite a particular episode, begin with the episode title, in quotation marks.

<u>Box Office Bombshell: Marilyn Monroe</u>. Writ. Andy Thomas, Jeff
        Schefel, and Kevin Burns. Dir. Bill Harris. Narr. Peter Graves.
        A&E Biography. Arts and Entertainment Network. 23 Oct. 2002.

"The Fleshy Part of the Thigh." <u>The Sopranos</u>. Writ. Diane Frolov and
        Andrew Schneider. Dir. Alan Taylor. HBO. 2 Apr. 2006.

Komando, Kim. "E-mail Hacking and the Law." <u>WCBS Radio</u>. WCBS,
        New York. 28 Oct. 2003. 11 Nov. 2003 <http://wcbs880.com/
        komando/local_story_309135535.html>.

65. SOUND RECORDING

Begin with the name of the person or group you wish to emphasize (such as the composer, conductor, or band). Then give the title
of the recording or musical composition; the artist(s), if appropriate;

the manufacturer; and the year of issue. If you are not citing a compact disc, give the medium (such as *MP3* or *LP*) before the manufacturer. If you are citing a particular song or selection, include its title, in quotation marks, before the title of the recording. If you are citing a piece of instrumental music (such as a symphony) that is identified only by form, number, and key, do not underline, italicize, or enclose it in quotation marks.

> Fountains of Wayne. "Bright Future in Sales." Welcome Interstate
> Managers. S-Curve, 2003.

> Grieg, Edvard. Concerto in A minor, op. 16. Cond. Eugene Ormandy.
> Philadelphia Orch. LP. RCA, 1989.

> Sonic Youth. "Incinerate." Rather Ripped. MP3. Geffen, 2006. 18
> June 2006 <http://www.sonicyouth.com/alt-main/rippedpop
> .html>.

66. MUSICAL COMPOSITION

When you are *not* citing a specific published version, first give the composer's name, followed by the title. Underline or italicize the title of an opera, a ballet, or a piece of instrumental music that is identified by name.

> Mozart, Wolfgang Amadeus. Don Giovanni, K527.

> Mozart, Wolfgang Amadeus. Symphony no. 41 in C major, K551.

Cite a published score as you would a book. If you include the date when the composition was written, do so immediately following the title.

> Schoenberg, Arnold. Chamber Symphony No. 1 for 15 Solo Instruments,
> Op. 9. 1906. New York: Dover, 2002.

67. LECTURE OR SPEECH

List the speaker, the title in quotation marks, the name of the sponsoring institution or group, the place, and the date. If the speech is untitled, use a label such as *Lecture* or *Keynote speech.*

Colbert, Stephen. Speech. White House Correspondents'
        Association Dinner. Washington Hilton, Washington, DC. 29
        Apr. 2006. 20 May 2006 <http://video.google.com/videoplay
        ?docid=-869183917758574879>.

Eugenides, Jeffrey. Lecture. Portland Arts and Lectures. Arlene
        Schnitzer Concert Hall, Portland, OR. 30 Sept. 2003.

68. LIVE PERFORMANCE

List the title, other appropriate details (composer, writer, performer, or director), the place, and the date. To cite a particular person's work, begin the entry with that name.

Anything Goes. By Cole Porter. Perf. Klea Blackhurst. Shubert Theater,
        New Haven. 7 Oct. 2003.

69. PODCAST

Include all of the following that are relevant and available: the speaker, the title of the podcast, the title of the program, the word *Podcast,* the host or performers, the title of the site, the date of posting, the site's sponsor, access information, and the URL. (Because the MLA currently provides no guidelines for documenting a podcast, this model is based on MLA guidelines for a short work from a Web site.)

"Seven Arrested in U.S. Terror Raid." Morning Report. Podcast.
        Host Krishnan Guru-Murthy. 4 Radio. 23 June 2006. Channel 4.

28 June 2006 <http://www.channel4.com/news/podcasts/
morning_report/mp3s/2006/06/23_mr.mp3>.

70. WORK OF ART OR PHOTOGRAPH

List the artist or photographer; the work's title, underlined or
italicized; the name of the museum or other location; and the city.
Add the publication information if you did not see the work in person.
If you want to include the date the work was created, add it after the
title.

Chagall, Marc. The Poet with the Birds. 1911. Minneapolis Inst. of
Arts. 6 Oct. 2003 <http://www.artsmia.org/collection/search/
art.cfm?id=1427>.

Kahlo, Frida. Self-Portrait with Cropped Hair. 1940. Museum of Mod.
Art, New York.

71. MAP OR CHART

Include the label *Map* or *Chart.*

Australia. Map. Perry-Castañeda Library Map Collection. 4 Nov. 2003
<http://www.lib.utexas.edu/maps/australia/australia_rel99.jpg>.

California. Map. Chicago: Rand, 2002.

72. CARTOON OR COMIC STRIP

List the artist's name; the title (if any) of the cartoon or comic
strip, in quotation marks; the label *Cartoon* or *Comic strip*; and the
usual publication information.

Johnston, Lynn. "For Better or for Worse." Comic strip. 30 June
2006. 20 July 2006 <http://www.fborfw.com/strip_fix/
archives/001879.php>.

Lewis, Eric. "The Unpublished Freud." Cartoon. <u>New Yorker</u> 11 Mar.

2002: 80.

73. ADVERTISEMENT

Include the label *Advertisement* after the name of the item or organization being advertised.

Microsoft. Advertisement. <u>Harper's</u> Oct. 2003: 2-3.

Microsoft. Advertisement. <u>New York Times Online</u> 11 Nov. 2003. 11

Nov. 2003 <http://www.nytimes.com/>.

A Student Research Essay, MLA Style

Student Writer

David Craig

On the following pages is an essay by David Craig that conforms to the MLA guidelines described in this chapter. Note that the essay has been reproduced in a narrow format to accommodate this book's pocket size.

David Craig

Professor Turkman

English 219

8 December 2003

Instant Messaging: The Language of Youth Literacy

The English language is under attack. At least, that
is what many people would have you believe. From
concerned parents to local librarians, everybody seems to
have a negative comment on the state of youth literacy
today, and many pin the blame on new technology. They
say that the current generation of grade school students
will graduate with an extremely low level of literacy and,
worse yet, that although language education hasn't
changed much, kids are having more trouble reading and
writing. Slang is more pervasive than ever, and teachers
often must struggle with students who refuse to learn
the conventionally correct way to use language.

In the Chronicle of Higher Education, for instance,
Wendy Leibowitz quotes Sven Birkerts of Mount Holyoke
College as saying "[Students] read more casually. They
strip-mine what they read" on the Internet. Those casual
reading habits, in turn, produce "quickly generated,
casual prose" (A67). When asked about the causes of this

situation, many point to instant messaging (IMing), which coincides with new computer technology.

Instant messaging allows two individuals who are separated by any distance to engage in real-time, written communication. Although IMing relies on the written word to transmit meaning, many messagers disregard standard writing conventions. For example, here is a snippet from an IM conversation between two teenage girls:[1]

> Teen One: sorry im talkinto like 10 ppl at a time
> Teen Two: u izzyful person
> Teen Two: kwel
> Teen One: hey i g2g

As this brief conversation shows, participants must use words to communicate via IMing, but their words do not have to be in standard English.

Instant messaging, according to many, threatens youth literacy because it creates and compounds

[1] This transcript of an IM conversation was collected on 20 Nov. 2003. The teenagers names are concealed to protect privacy.

Craig 3

undesirable reading and writing habits and discourages
students from learning standard literacy skills. Passionate
or not, however, the critics' arguments don't hold up. In
fact, instant messaging seems to be a beneficial force in
the development of youth literacy because it promotes
regular contact with words, the use of a written medium
for communication, and the development of an
alternative form of literacy. Perhaps most important,
IMing can actually help students learn conventional
English. Before turning to the pros and cons of IMing,
however, I wish to look more closely at two background
issues: the current state of literacy and the prevalence of
IMing.

Regardless of one's views on IMing, the issue of
youth literacy does demand attention because
standardized test scores for language assessments, such
as the verbal section of the College Board's SAT, have
declined in recent years. This trend is illustrated in a
chart distributed by the College Board as part of its 2002
analysis of aggregate SAT data (see Fig. 1).

The trend lines, which I added to the original chart,
illustrate a significant pattern that may lead to the
conclusion that youth literacy is on the decline. These

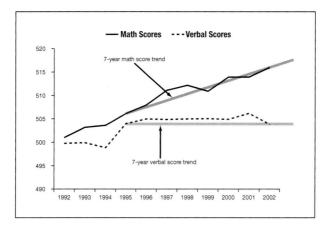

Fig. 1. Comparison of SAT math and verbal scores (1992-2002), from Kristin Carnahan and Chiara Coletti, Ten-Year Trend in SAT Scores Indicates Increased Emphasis on Math Is Yielding results; Reading and Writing Are Causes for Concern (New York: College Board, 2002) 9. Trend lines added.

lines display the seven-year paths (from 1995 to 2002) of math and verbal scores, respectively. Within this time period, the average SAT math score jumped more than ten points. The average verbal score, however, actually dropped a few points--and appears to be headed toward a further decline in the future. Corroborating this evidence is a report from the United States Department of Education's National Center for Education Statistics. According to this agency's study, the percentage of twelfth graders whose writing ability was "at or above the basic level" of performance dropped from 78 to 74 percent between 1998 and 2002 (Persky, Daane, and Jin 21).

Based on the preceding statistics, parents and educators appear to be right about the decline in youth literacy. And this trend is occurring while IM usage is on the rise. According to the Pew Internet and American Life Project, 54 percent of American youths aged twelve to seventeen have used IMing (qtd. in Lenhart and Lewis 20). This figure translates to a pool of some thirteen million young instant messagers. Of this group, Pew reports, half send instant messages every time they go online, with 46 percent spending between thirty and sixty minutes messaging and another 21 percent spending more than an hour. The most conservative estimate indicates that American youths spend, at a minimum, nearly three million hours per day on IMing. What's more, they seem to be using a new vocabulary, and this is one of the things that bothers critics. In order to have an effect on youth literacy, however, this new vocabulary must actually exist, so I set out to determine if it did.

In the interest of establishing the existence of IM language, I analyzed 11,341 lines of text from IM conversations between youths in my target demographic: US residents aged twelve to seventeen. Young messagers voluntarily sent me chat logs, but they were unaware of the exact nature of my research. Once all of the logs had been gathered, I went through them, recording the number of times IM language was used in place of conventional words and phrases. Then I generated graphs to display how often these replacements were used.

During the course of my study, I identified four types of IM language: phonetic replacements, acronyms, abbreviations, and inanities. An example of phonetic replacement is using ur for you are. Another popular type of IM language is the acronym; for a majority of the people in my study, the most common acronym was lol, a construction that means laughing out loud. Abbreviations are also common in IMing, but I discovered that typical IM abbreviations, such as etc., are not new to the English language. Finally, I found a class of words that I call "inanities." These words include completely new words or expressions, combinations of several slang categories, or simply nonsensical variations of other words. My favorite from this category is lolz, an inanity that translates directly to lol yet includes a terminating z for no obvious reason.

In the chat transcripts that I analyzed, the best display of typical IM lingo came from the conversations between two thirteen-year-old Texan girls, who are avid IM users. Figure 2 is a graph showing how often they used certain phonetic replacements and abbreviations. On the y-axis, frequency of replacement is plotted, a calculation that compares the number of times a word or phrase is used in IM language with the total number of times that it is communicated in any form. On the x-axis, specific IM words and phrases are listed.

My research shows that the Texan girls use the first ten phonetic replacements or abbreviations at least 50 percent of the time in their normal IM writing. For example, every time one of them writes see, there is a parallel time when c is used in its place. In light of this finding, it appears that the popular IM culture contains at least some elements of its own language. It also

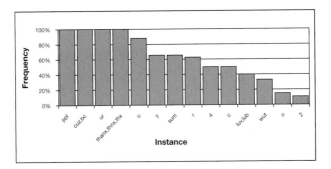

Fig. 2. Usage of phonetic replacements and abbreviations in IMing.

seems that much of this language is new: no formal dictionary yet identifies the most common IM words and phrases. Only in the heyday of the telegraph or on the rolls of a stenographer would you find a similar situation, but these "languages" were never a popular medium of youth communication. Instant messaging, however, is very popular among young people and continues to generate attention and debate in academic circles.

My research shows that messaging is certainly widespread, and it does seem to have its own particular vocabulary, yet these two factors alone do not mean it has a damaging influence on youth literacy. As noted earlier, however, some people claim that the new technology is a threat to the English language, as revealed in the following passage:

> Abbreviations commonly used in online instant messages are creeping into formal essays that students write for credit, said Debbie Frost, who teaches language arts and social studies to sixth-graders. . . . "You would be shocked at the writing I see. It's pretty scary. I don't get cohesive thoughts, I don't get sentences, they don't capitalize, and they have a lot of misspellings and bad grammar," she said. "With all those glaring mistakes, it's hard to see the content." ("Young Messagers," par. 2)

Echoing Frost's concerns is Melanie Weaver, a professor at Alvernia College, who taught a tenth-grade English class as an intern. In an interview with the New York Times, she said, "[When t]hey would be trying to make a point in a paper, they would put a smiley face in the end [:)]. . . . If they were presenting an argument and they needed to present an opposite view, they would put a frown [:(]" (qtd. in Lee, par. 11).

The critics of instant messaging are numerous. But if we look to the field of linguistics, a central concept-- metalinguistics--challenges these criticisms and leads to a more reasonable conclusion--that IMing has no negative impact on a student's development of or proficiency with traditional literacy.

Scholars of metalinguistics offer support for the claim that IMing is not damaging to those who use it. As noted earlier, one of the most prominent components of IM language is phonetic replacement, in which a word such as everyone becomes every1. This type of wordplay has a special importance in the development of an advanced literacy, and for good reason. According to David Crystal, an internationally recognized scholar of linguistics at the University of Wales, as young children develop and learn how words string together to express ideas, they go through many phases of language play. The singsong rhymes and nonsensical chants of preschoolers are vital to their learning language, and a healthy appetite for such wordplay leads to a better command of language later in life (182).

As justification for his view of the connection between language play and advanced literacy, Crystal presents an argument for metalinguistic awareness. According to Crystal, metalinguistics refers to the ability to "step back" and use words to analyze how language works. "If we are good at stepping back," he says, "at thinking in a more abstract way about what we hear and what we say, then we are more likely to be good at acquiring those skills which depend on just such a stepping back in order to be successful--and this means, chiefly, reading and writing. . . . [T]he greater our ability to play with language, . . . the more advanced will be our command of language as a whole" (181).

If we accept the findings of linguists such as Crystal that metalinguistic awareness leads to increased literacy, then it seems reasonable to argue that the phonetic language of IMing can also lead to increased meta-linguistic awareness and, therefore, increases in overall literacy. As instant messengers develop proficiency with a variety of phonetic replacements and other types of IM words, they should increase their subconscious knowledge of metalinguistics.

Metalinguistics also involves our ability to write in a variety of distinct styles and tones. Yet in the debate over instant messaging and literacy, many critics assume

Craig 12

that either IMing or academic literacy will eventually win out in a person and that the two modes cannot exist side by side. This assumption is, however, false. Human beings ordinarily develop a large range of language abilities, from the formal to the relaxed and from the mainstream to the subcultural. Mark Twain, for example, had an understanding of local speech that he employed when writing dialogue for Huckleberry Finn. Yet few people would argue that Twain's knowledge of this form of English had a negative impact on his ability to write in standard English.

However, just as Mark Twain used dialects carefully in dialogue, writers must pay careful attention to the kind of language they use in any setting. The owner of the language Web site The Discouraging Word (http://www.thediscouragingword.com), who is an anonymous English literature graduate student at the University of Chicago, backs up this idea in an e-mail to me:

> What is necessary, we feel, is that students
> learn how to shift between different styles of
> writing--that, in other words, the abbreviations
> and shortcuts of IM should be used online . . .
> but that they should not be used in an essay

submitted to a teacher. . . . IM might even be
considered . . . a different way of reading and
writing, one that requires specific and unique
skills shared by certain communities.

The analytical ability that is necessary for writers to
choose an appropriate tone and style in their writing is,
of course, metalinguistic in nature because it involves
the comparison of two or more language systems. Thus,
youths who grasp multiple languages will have a greater
natural understanding of metalinguistics. More
specifically, young people who possess both IM and
traditional skills stand to be better off than their peers
who have been trained only in traditional or
conventional systems. Far from being hurt by their online
pastime, instant messagers can be aided in standard
writing by their experience with IM language.

The fact remains, however, that youth literacy seems
to be declining. What, if not IMing, is the main cause of
this phenomenon? According to the College Board, which
collects data on several questions from its test takers,
enrollment in English composition and grammar classes
has decreased in the last decade by 14 percent
(Carnahan and Coletti 11). The possibility of instant

messaging causing a decline in literacy seems inadequate when statistics on English education for US youths provide other evidence of the possible causes. Simply put, schools in the United States are not teaching English as much as they used to. Rather than blaming IMing alone for the decline in literacy and test scores, we must also look toward our schools' lack of focus on the teaching of standard English skills.

I found that the use of instant messaging poses virtually no threat to the development or maintenance of formal language skills among American youths aged twelve to seventeen. Diverse language skills tend to increase a person's metalinguistic awareness and, thereby, his or her ability to use language effectively to achieve a desired purpose in a particular situation. The current decline in youth literacy is not due to the rise of instant messaging. Rather, fewer young students seem to be receiving an adequate education in the use of conventional English. Unfortunately, it may always be fashionable to blame new tools for old problems, but in the case of instant messaging, that blame is not warranted. Although IMing may expose literacy problems, it does not create them.

Works Cited

Carnahan, Kristin, and Chiara Coletti. Ten-Year Trend in SAT Scores Indicates Increased Emphasis on Math Is Yielding Results; Reading and Writing Are Causes for Concern. New York: College Board, 2002.

Crystal, David. Language Play. Chicago: U of Chicago P, 1998.

The Discouraging Word. "Re: Instant Messaging and Literacy." E-mail to the author. 13 Nov. 2003.

Lee, Jennifer 8. "I Think, Therefore IM." New York Times Online 19 Sept. 2002. 14 Nov. 2003 <http://www.nytimes.com/2002/09/19/technology/circuits>.

Leibowitz, Wendy R. "Technology Transforms Writing and the Teaching of Writing." Chronicle of Higher Education 26 Nov. 1999: A67-68.

Lenhart, Amanda, and Oliver Lewis. Teenage Life Online: The Rise of the Instant-Message Generation and the Internet's Impact on Friendships and Family Relationships. Washington: Pew Internet and Amer. Life Project, 2001.

Persky, Hilary R., Mary C. Daane, and Ying Jin. The Nation's Report Card: Writing 2002. NCES 2003-529. Washington: GPO, 2003.

Craig 16

"Young Messagers Ask: Why Spell It Out?" _Associated Press State and Local Wire_ 11 Nov. 2002. 14 Nov. 2003 <http://www.lexis-nexis.com>.

Chicago Style

The Fifteenth Edition of *The Chicago Manual of Style,* published in 2003, provides a complete guide to the system of documentation known as *Chicago* style, which has long been used in history and some other fields in the humanities, as well as in publishing.

For further reference, consult *The Chicago Manual* or a volume intended specifically for student writers, Kate L. Turabian's *A Manual for Writers of Term Papers, Theses, and Dissertations,* Sixth Edition (1996).

Chicago Format for In-Text Citations, Notes, and Bibliography

In *Chicago* style, use superscript numbers (^{1}) to mark citations in the text. Sequentially numbered citations throughout the text correspond to notes that contain either publication information about the source cited or explanatory or supplemental material not included in the main text. Place the superscript material for each note near the cited material — at the end of the relevant quotation, sentence, clause, or phrase. Type the number after any punctuation mark except the dash, and leave no space between the superscript and the preceding letter or punctuation mark. When you use signal phrases to introduce quotations or other source material, note that *Chicago* style requires you to use the present tense (*citing Bebout's studies, Meier points out*).

The notes themselves can be footnotes (each typed at the bottom of the page on which the superscript for it appears in the text) or endnotes (all typed on a separate page at the end of the text under the heading *Notes*). Be sure to check your instructor's preference. The first line of each note is indented like a paragraph (three to five spaces) and begins with a number followed by a period, one space, and the first word. All remaining lines of the entry are typed flush with the left margin. Footnotes and endnotes should be double-spaced.

IN THE TEXT

Sweig argues that Castro and Che Guevara were not the only key players in the Cuban Revolution of the late 1950s.[19]

IN THE FIRST NOTE

19. Julia Sweig, *Inside the Cuban Revolution* (Cambridge, MA: Harvard University Press, 2002), 9.

After giving complete information the first time you cite a work, shorten any additional references to that work: list only the author's last name followed by a comma, a shortened version of the title, a comma, and the page number. If the reference is to the same source cited in the previous note, you can use the Latin abbreviation *Ibid.* (for "in the same place") instead of the name and title.

IN SUBSEQUENT NOTES

19. Julia Sweig, *Inside the Cuban Revolution* (Cambridge, MA: Harvard University Press, 2002), 9.

20. Ibid., 13.

21. Ferguson, "Comfort of Being Sad," 63.

22. Sweig, *Cuban Revolution,* 21.

The alphabetical list of the sources in your paper is usually titled *Bibliography* in *Chicago* style. You may instead use the title *Sources Consulted, Works Cited,* or *Selected Bibliography* if it better describes your list.

In the bibliographic entry for a source, include the same information as in the first note for that source, but omit the specific page reference. However, give the *first* author's last name first, followed by a comma and the first name; separate the main elements of the entry with periods rather than commas; and do not enclose the publication information for books in parentheses. Type the first line flush with the left margin, and indent the subsequent lines of each entry three to five spaces.

IN THE BIBLIOGRAPHY

Sweig, Julia. *Inside the Cuban Revolution*. Cambridge, MA: Harvard University Press, 2002.

Start the bibliography on a separate page after the main text and any endnotes. Continue the consecutive numbering of pages. Center the title *Bibliography* (without underlining, italics, or quotation marks) one inch below the top of the page. List sources alphabetically by authors' last names or, if an author is unknown, by the first major word in the title. Double-space the entire list.

DIRECTORY TO *CHICAGO* STYLE

BOOKS

PERIODICALS

(Continued)

Chicago Format for Notes and Bibliographic Entries

The following examples demonstrate how to format both notes and bibliographic entries according to *Chicago* style. The note, which is numbered, appears first; the bibliographic entry, which is not numbered, appears below the note.

Books

For the basic format for citing a book in *Chicago* style, see pp. 136–37. The note for a book typically includes four elements: the author's name, the title and subtitle, the publication information, and the page number(s) to which the note refers. The bibliographic entry for a book usually includes the first three of these elements, but they are styled somewhat differently.

1. ONE AUTHOR

1. James S. Hirsch, *Riot and Remembrance: The Tulsa Race War and Its Legacy* (Boston: Houghton Mifflin, 2002), 119.

Hirsch, James S. *Riot and Remembrance: The Tulsa Race War and Its Legacy.* Boston: Houghton Mifflin, 2002.

2. MULTIPLE AUTHORS

2. Margaret Macmillan and Richard Holbrooke, *Paris 1919: Six Months That Changed the World* (New York: Random House, 2003), 384.

Macmillan, Margaret, and Richard Holbrooke. *Paris 1919: Six Months That Changed the World.* New York: Random House, 2003.

When there are more than three authors, you may give the first-listed author followed by *et al.* or *and others* in the note. In the bibliography, however, list all the authors' names.

2. Stephen J. Blank and others, *Conflict, Culture, and History: Regional Dimensions* (Miami: University Press of the Pacific, 2002), 276.

Blank, Stephen J., Lawrence E. Grinter, Karl P. Magyar, Lewis B. Ware, and Bynum E. Weathers. *Conflict, Culture, and History: Regional Dimensions.* Miami: University Press of the Pacific, 2002.

3. ORGANIZATION AS AUTHOR

3. World Intellectual Property Organization, *Intellectual Property Profile of the Least Developed Countries* (Geneva: World Intellectual Property Organization, 2002), 43.

World Intellectual Property Organization. *Intellectual Property Profile of the Least Developed Countries.* Geneva: World Intellectual Property Organization, 2002.

4. UNKNOWN AUTHOR

4. *Broad Stripes and Bright Stars* (Kansas City, MO: Andrews McMeel, 2002), 10.

Broad Stripes and Bright Stars. Kansas City, MO: Andrews McMeel,
    2002.

5. EDITOR

5. James H. Fetzer, ed., *The Great Zapruder Film Hoax:
Deceit and Deception in the Death of JFK* (Chicago: Open Court,
2003), 56.

Fetzer, James H., ed. *The Great Zapruder Film Hoax: Deceit and
    Deception in the Death of JFK.* Chicago: Open Court,
    2003.

6. SELECTION IN AN ANTHOLOGY OR CHAPTER IN A BOOK, WITH AN EDITOR

6. Denise Little, "Born in Blood," in *Alternate Gettysburgs,*
ed. Brian Thomsen and Martin H. Greenberg (New York: Berkley
Publishing Group, 2002), 245.

Give the inclusive page numbers of the selection or chapter in the bibliographic entry.

Little, Denise. "Born in Blood." In Alternate *Gettysburgs,* edited
    by Brian Thomsen and Martin H. Greenberg, 242–55. New York:
    Berkley Publishing Group, 2002.

7. TRANSLATION

7. Suetonius, *The Twelve Caesars,* trans. Robert Graves
(London: Penguin Classics, 1989), 202.

Suetonius. *The Twelve Caesars.* Translated by Robert Graves.
    London: Penguin Classics, 1989.

SOURCE MAP: Citing books using *Chicago* style

Take information from the book's title page and copyright page (on the reverse side of the title page), not from the book's cover or a library catalog.

(1) *Author.* In a note, list author first name first. In a bibliographic entry, list the first author last name first, followed by a comma; list other authors first name first.

(2) *Title.* Italicize title and subtitle, and capitalize major words. In a note, put a comma before the title. In the bibliography, place a period before and after the title.

(3) *City of publication.* List the city (and country or state abbreviation for an unfamiliar city) followed by a colon. In a note only, city, publisher, and year appear in parentheses.

(4) *Publisher.* Drop *Inc.*, *Co.*, *Publishing*, or *Publishers*. Follow with a comma.

(5) *Publication year.* In a note, end with parentheses, comma, page number, and period. In the bibliography, end with a period.

For a book by one author, use the following formats:

Endnote

   Note number. First name Last name, *Title of Book* (City: Publisher, Year), Page number(s).

Bibliographic entry

Last name, First name. *Title of Book*. City: Publisher, Year.

Citations for the book on p. 137 would look like this:

Endnote

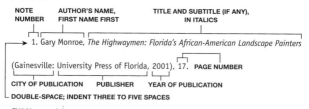

Bibliographic entry

Monroe, Gary. *The Highwaymen: Florida's African-American Landscape Painters.*

   Gainesville: University Press of Florida, 2001.

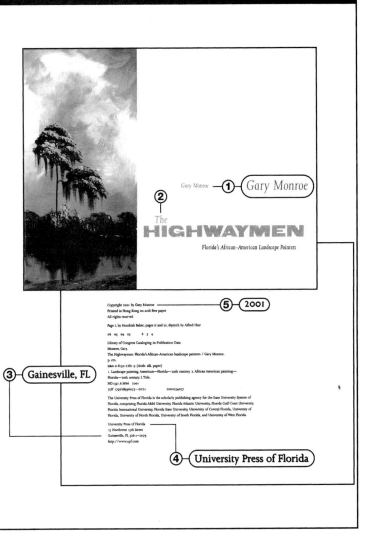

Gary Monroe — (1) — Gary Monroe

(2)

The
HIGHWAYMEN

Florida's African-American Landscape Painters

Copyright 2001 by Gary Monroe — (5) — 2001
Printed in Hong Kong on acid-free paper
All rights reserved

Page i, by Hezekiah Baker; pages ii and iii, diptych by Alfred Hair

06 05 04 03   6 5 4

Library of Congress Cataloging-in-Publication Data
Monroe, Gary.
The Highwaymen: Florida's African-American landscape painters / Gary Monroe.
p. cm.
ISBN 0-8130-2181-9 (cloth: alk. paper)
1. Landscape painting, American—Florida—20th century. 2. African American painting—
Florida—20th century. I. Title.

(3) — Gainesville, FL

ND1351.6.M66   2001
758'.1759'08996073—DC21   2001034077

The University Press of Florida is the scholarly publishing agency for the State University System of
Florida, comprising Florida A&M University, Florida Atlantic University, Florida Gulf Coast University,
Florida International University, Florida State University, University of Central Florida, University of
Florida, University of North Florida, University of South Florida, and University of West Florida.

University Press of Florida
15 Northwest 15th Street
Gainesville, FL 32611-2079
http://www.upf.com

(4) — University Press of Florida

8. EDITION OTHER THAN THE FIRST

8. Charles G. Beaudette, *Excess Heat: Why Cold Fusion Research Prevailed,* 2nd ed. (South Bristol, ME: Oak Grove Press, 2002), 313.

Beaudette, Charles G. *Excess Heat: Why Cold Fusion Research Prevailed*. 2nd ed. South Bristol, ME: Oak Grove Press, 2002.

9. MULTIVOLUME WORK

9. John Watson, *Annals of Philadelphia and Pennsylvania in the Olden Time,* vol. 2 (Washington, DC: Ross & Perry, 2003), 514.

Watson, John. *Annals of Philadelphia and Pennsylvania in the Olden Time*. Vol. 2. Washington, DC: Ross & Perry, 2003.

10. REFERENCE WORK

In a note, use *s.v.,* the abbreviation for the Latin *sub verbo* ("under the word") to help your reader find the entry.

10. *Encarta World Dictionary,* s.v. "carpetbagger."

Do not list reference works in your bibliography.

Periodicals

For the basic format for citing an article from a periodical in *Chicago* style, see pp. 140–41. The note for an article in a periodical typically includes the author's name, the article title, and the periodical title. The format for other information, including the volume and issue numbers (if any), the date of publication, and the page number(s) to which the note refers, varies according to the type of periodical. In a bibliographic entry for an article from a periodical, also give the inclusive page numbers.

11. ARTICLE IN A JOURNAL PAGINATED BY VOLUME

11. Linda Hutcheon, "She Do the President in Different Voices," PMLA 116 (2001): 518.

Hutcheon, Linda. "She Do the President in Different Voices." PMLA 116 (2001): 518.

12. ARTICLE IN A JOURNAL PAGINATED BY ISSUE

12. Karin Lützen, "The Female World: Viewed from Denmark," *Journal of Women's History* 12, no. 3 (2000): 36.

Lützen, Karin. "The Female World: Viewed from Denmark." *Journal of Women's History* 12, no. 3 (2000): 34–38.

13. ARTICLE IN A MAGAZINE

13. Douglas Brinkley and Anne Brinkley, "Lawyers and Lizard-Heads," *Atlantic Monthly,* May 2002, 56.

Brinkley, Douglas, and Anne Brinkley. "Lawyers and Lizard-Heads." *Atlantic Monthly,* May 2002, 55–61.

14. ARTICLE IN A NEWSPAPER

14. Caroline E. Mayer, "Wireless Industry to Adopt Voluntary Standards," *Washington Post,* September 9, 2003, sec. E.

Mayer, Caroline E. "Wireless Industry to Adopt Voluntary Standards." *Washington Post,* September 9, 2003, sec. E.

Electronic Sources

15. ARTICLE FROM A DATABASE

For the basic format for citing an article from a database in *Chicago* style, see pp. 142–43.

SOURCE MAP: Citing articles from periodicals using *Chicago* style

① *Author.* In a note, list author first name first. In a bibliographic entry, list the first author last name first, comma, first name; list other authors' names first name first.

② *Article title.* Enclose title and subtitle (if any) in quotation marks, and capitalize major words. In the notes section, put a comma before and after the title. In the bibliography, put a period before and after.

③ *Periodical title.* Italicize title and subtitle and capitalize major words. Follow the title with a comma, unless it is a journal.

④ *Journal volume and issue numbers.* For journals only, include the volume number, a comma, the abbreviation *no.*, and the issue number.

⑤ *Publication date.* For journals, enclose the publication year in parentheses and follow with a colon. For other periodicals, give the month and year or the month, day, and year followed by a comma.

⑥ *Page numbers.* In the notes section, give the page number. In the bibliography, give inclusive page numbers. For newspapers, write *sec.* and give the section number or letter. End with a period.

For a magazine article by one author, use the following formats:

Endnote

    1. First name Last name, "Title of Article," *Title of Magazine*, month year or month day, year, page number(s).

Bibliographic entry

Last name, First name. "Title of Article." *Title of Magazine*, month year or month day, year, page number(s).

Citations for the magazine article on p. 141 would look like this:

Endnote

NOTE NUMBER	AUTHOR'S NAME, FIRST NAME FIRST		MAGAZINE TITLE, ITALICIZED	PAGE NUMBER

→ 1. John Hockenberry, "The Blogs of War," *Wired*, August 2005, 118.

ARTICLE TITLE, IN QUOTATION MARKS   PUBLICATION DATE

INDENT THREE TO FIVE SPACES

Bibliographic entry

Hockenberry, John. "The Blogs of War." *Wired*, August 2005, 118–35.

② THE BLOGS OF WAR

① BY JOHN HOCKENBERRY

③ • WIRED

⑤ 08|2005

⑥ 118

SOURCE MAP: Citing articles from databases using *Chicago* style

(1) *Author.* In a note, list author first name first. In the bibliographic entry, list the first author last name first, comma, first name; list other authors first name first.

(2) *Article title.* Enclose title and subtitle (if any) in quotation marks, and capitalize major words. In the notes section, put a comma before and after the title. In the bibliography, put a period before and after.

(3) *Periodical title.* Italicize the title and subtitle, and capitalize all major words. Follow with a comma, unless it is a journal.

(4) *Journal volume and issue numbers.* For journals, follow the title with the volume number, a comma, the abbreviation *no.*, and the issue number.

(5) *Publication date.* For journals, enclose the publication year in parentheses and follow with a comma (in a note) or with a period (in a bibliography). For other periodicals, give the month and year or month, day, and year, followed by a comma.

(6) *Retrieval information.* Give the brief URL for the database, followed, in parentheses, by the word *accessed* and the access date. End with a period.

For an article accessed from a database, use the following formats:

Endnote

    1. First name Last name, "Title of Article," *Periodical Title* Volume, no. Issue (Year), Database URL (accessed Date).

Bibliographic entry

Last name, First name. "Title of Article." *Periodical Title* Volume, no. Issue (Year).
    Database URL (accessed Date).

Citations for the article on p. 143 would look like this:

Endnote

NOTE NUMBER	AUTHORS' NAMES	ARTICLE TITLE, IN QUOTATION MARKS

1. Howard Schuman, Barry Schwartz, and Hannah D'Arcy, "Elite Revisionists and

PERIODICAL TITLE, ITALICIZED

Popular Beliefs: Christopher Columbus, Hero or Villain?" *Public Opinion Quarterly*

69, no. 1 (2005), http://elibrary.bigchalk.com (accessed October 15, 2005).

VOLUME NUMBER;   PUBLICATION   DATABASE URL   DATE OF
ISSUE NUMBER (IF GIVEN)   DATE   ACCESS

DOUBLE-SPACE ENTRY; INDENT THREE TO FIVE SPACES

Bibliographic entry

Schuman, Howard, Barry Schwartz, and Hannah D'Arcy. "Elite Revisionists
and Popular Beliefs: Christopher Columbus, Hero or Villain?" *Public
Opinion Quarterly* 69, no. 1 (2005). http://elibrary.bigchalk.com
(accessed October 15, 2005).

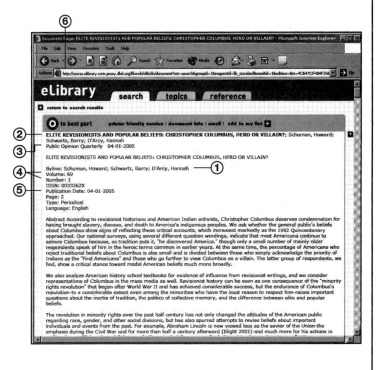

SOURCE MAP: Citing works from Web sites using *Chicago* style

(1) *Author.* In a note, list author first name first. In a bibliographic entry, list the first author last name first, comma, first name; list additional authors first name first. Note that the host may serve as the author.

(2) *Document title.* Enclose the title in quotation marks, and capitalize all major words. In a note, put a comma before and after the title. In the bibliography, put a period before and after.

(3) *Title of Web site.* Italicize the title and capitalize all major words. In the notes section, put a comma after the title. In the bibliography, put a period after the title.

(4) *Retrieval information.* Give the URL for the Website, followed, in parentheses, by the word *accessed* and the access date. End with a period.

When citing works from Web sites, use the following formats:

Endnote

1. First name Last name, "Title of Document," *Title of Web Site*, URL (accessed date).

Bibliographic entry

Last name, First name. "Title of Document." *Title of Web Site*. URL (accessed date).

Citations for the Web site on p. 145 would look like this:

Endnote

NOTE NUMBER	AUTHOR'S NAME, FIRST NAME FIRST	DOCUMENT TITLE, IN QUOTATION MARKS	TITLE OF WEB SITE, IN ITALICS

→ 1. Douglas Linder, "The Scopes Trial: An Introduction," *Famous Trials, University of Missouri-Kansas City School of Law,* http://www.law.umkc.edu/faculty/projects/ FTrials/scopes/scopes.htm (accessed September 24, 2006). — RETRIEVAL INFORMATION

└─ INDENT THREE TO FIVE SPACES

Bibliographic entry

Linder, Douglas. "The Scopes Trial: An Introduction." *Famous Trials, University of Missouri-Kansas City School of Law*. http://www.law.umkc.edu/faculty/projects/ FTrials/scopes/scopes.htm (accessed September 24, 2006).

(4) http://www.law.umkc.edu/faculty/projects/FTrials/scopes/scopes.htm

Scopes Trial Home Page - UMKC School of Law - Microsoft Internet Explorer

File   Edit   View   Favorites   Tools   Help

Address http://www.law.umkc.edu/faculty/projects/FTrials/scopes/scopes.htm   Go   Links

Anti-Evolution Statute
Genesis Stories
Excerpts from Scopes Trial Transcript
Observer's Account
Mencken's Trial Account
Biographies of Key Figures
Text Used by Scopes
Dayton, Tennessee
Trial Pictures and Cartoons
Darrow Page
Appellate Decisions
Scopes Trial Satire
Chronology & Year 1925
Trial of the Century?
Evolution Controversy
Inherit the Wind
Expert's Impressions
John Scopes Reflects
Hell & High Schools
Links & Bibliography
Trial Video
Trial Jeopardy
Send Comments

Famous Trials in American History

Tennessee vs. John Scopes
The "Monkey Trial"

1925

Clarence Darrow and William Jennings Bryan during the trial
Photo Credit: CORBIS/Bettmann

(2)— The Scopes Trial: An Introduction

by Douglas Linder (c) 2002

The early 1920s found social patterns in chaos. Traditionalists, the older Victorians, worried that everything valuable was ending. Younger modernists no longer asked whether society would approve of their behavior, only whether their behavior met the approval of their intellect. Intellectual experimentation flourished. Americans danced to the sound of the Jazz Age, showed their contempt for alcoholic prohibition, debated abstract art and Freudian theories. In a response to the new social patterns set in motion by modernism, a wave of revivalism developed, becoming especially strong in the American South.   (1)— *by Douglas Linder*

Who would dominate American culture--the modernists or the traditionalists? Jour... showdown, and they found one in a Dayton, Tennessee courtroom in the summer of 1925...[CONTINUED]

Famous Trials Homepage ——— (3)

THIS SITE LAST UPDATED 4/25/05

Internet

15. Peter DeMarco, "Holocaust Survivors Lend Voice to History," *Boston Globe,* November 2, 2003, http://www.lexisnexis.com (accessed November 19, 2003).

DeMarco, Peter. "Holocaust Survivors Lend Voice to History." *Boston Globe,* November 2, 2003. http://www.lexisnexis.com (accessed November 19, 2003).

16. ONLINE BOOK

16. Janja Bec, *The Shattering of the Soul* (Los Angeles: Simon Wiesenthal Center, 1997), http://motlc.wiesenthal.com/resources/books/shatteringsoul/index.html (accessed November 6, 2005).

Bec, Janja. *The Shattering of the Soul.* Los Angeles: Simon Wiesenthal Center, 1997. http://motlc.wiesenthal.com/resources/books/shatteringsoul/index.html (accessed November 6, 2005).

17. ARTICLE IN AN ELECTRONIC JOURNAL

17. Damian Bracken, "Rationalism and the Bible in Seventh-Century Ireland," *Chronicon* 2 (1998), http://www.ucc.ie/chronicon/bracfra.htm (accessed November 1, 2004).

Bracken, Damian. "Rationalism and the Bible in Seventh-Century Ireland." *Chronicon* 2 (1998). http://www.ucc.ie/chronicon/bracfra.htm (accessed November 1, 2004).

If a scholarly journal has both print and online versions and page numbers are shown online, give the inclusive pages of the article, after the publication date, in the bibliographic reference only: *(May 2006): 432–58.*

18. ARTICLE IN AN ONLINE MAGAZINE

18. Kim Iskyan, "Putin's Next Power Play," *Slate,* November 4, 2003, http://slate.msn.com/id/2090745 (accessed November 7, 2005).

Iskyan, Kim. "Putin's Next Power Play." *Slate,* November 4, 2003. http://slate.msn.com/id/2090745 (accessed November 7, 2005).

19. ARTICLE FROM A WEB SITE

For the basic format for citing an article from a Web site, see pp. 144–45.

19. Rutgers University, "Picture Gallery," *The Rutgers Oral History Archives of World War II,* http://fas-history.rutgers.edu/oralhistory/orlhom.htm (accessed January 17, 2006).

Rutgers University. "Picture Gallery." *The Rutgers Oral History Archives of World War II.* http://fas-history.rutgers.edu/oralhistory/orlhom.htm (accessed January 17, 2006).

20. EMAIL AND OTHER PERSONAL COMMUNICATIONS

Cite email messages and other personal communications, such as letters and telephone calls, in the text or in a note only, not in the bibliography. (*Chicago* style recommends hyphenating *e-mail.*)

20. Kareem Adas, e-mail message to author, February 11, 2006.

Other Sources

21. PUBLISHED OR BROADCAST INTERVIEW

21. Condoleezza Rice, interview by Charlie Rose, *The Charlie Rose Show,* PBS, October 30, 2003.

Rice, Condoleezza. Interview by Charlie Rose. *The Charlie Rose Show*.
PBS, October 30, 2003.

Interviews you conduct are considered personal communications.

22. VIDEO OR DVD

22. Edward Norton and Edward Furlong, *American History X,*
DVD, directed by Tony Kaye (1998; Los Angeles: New Line Studios,
2002).

Norton, Edward, and Edward Furlong. *American History X*. DVD.
Directed by Tony Kaye, 1998. Los Angeles: New Line Studios,
2002.

23. CD-ROM

23. *The Civil War,* CD-ROM (Fogware, 2000).

The Civil War. CD-ROM. Fogware, 2000.

24. PAMPHLET, REPORT, OR BROCHURE

Information about the author or publisher may not be readily
available, but give enough information to identify your source.

24. Jamie McCarthy, *Who Is David Irving?* (San Antonio, TX:
Holocaust History Project, 1998).

McCarthy, Jamie. *Who Is David Irving?* San Antonio, TX: Holocaust
History Project, 1998.

25. GOVERNMENT DOCUMENT

25. U.S. House Committee on Ways and Means, *Report on Trade Mission to Sub-Saharan Africa,* 108th Cong., 1st sess. (Washington, DC: U.S. Government Printing Office, 2003), 28.

U.S. House Committee on Ways and Means. *Report on Trade Mission to Sub-Saharan Africa.* 108th Cong., 1st sess. Washington, DC: U.S. Government Printing Office, 2003.

A Student Research Essay, *Chicago* Style

On the following pages is an essay by Amanda Rinder that conforms to the *Chicago* guidelines described in this chapter. Note that the essay has been reproduced in a narrow format to accommodate the book's pocket size.

Student Writer

Amanda Rinder

Sweet Home Chicago: Preserving the Past,
Protecting the Future of the Windy City
Amanda Rinder

Twentieth-Century U.S. History
Professor Goldberg
November 27, 2006

Only one city has the "Big Shoulders" described by Carl Sandburg: Chicago (fig. 1). So renowned are its skyscrapers and celebrated building style that an entire school of architecture is named for Chicago. Presently, however, the place that Frank Sinatra called "my kind of town" is beginning to lose sight of exactly what kind of town it is. Many of the buildings that give Chicago its distinctive character are being torn down in order to make room for new growth. Both preserving the classics

Fig. 1. Chicago skyline, circa 1940s. (Postcard courtesy of Minnie Dangberg.)

and encouraging new creation are important; the combination of these elements gives Chicago architecture its unique flavor. Witold Rybczynski, a professor of urbanism at the University of Pennsylvania, told the *New York Times,* "Of all the cities we can think of . . . we associate Chicago with new things, with building new. Combining that with preservation is a difficult task, a tricky thing. It's hard to find the middle ground in Chicago."[1] Yet finding a middle ground is essential if the city is to retain the original character that sets it apart from the rest. In order to maintain Chicago's distinctive identity and its delicate balance between the old and the new, the city government must provide a comprehensive urban plan that not only directs growth, but calls for the preservation of landmarks and historic districts as well.

Chicago is a city for the working man. Nowhere is this more evident than in its architecture. David Garrard Lowe, author of *Lost Chicago,* notes that early Chicagoans "sought reality, not fantasy, and the reality of America as seen from the heartland did not include the pavilions of princes or the castles of kings."[2] The inclination toward unadorned, sturdy buildings began in the late nineteenth century with the aptly named Chicago School, a

movement led by Louis Sullivan, John Wellborn Root, and
Daniel Burnham and based on Sullivan's adage, "Form
follows function."[3] Burnham and Root's Reliance Building
(fig. 2) epitomizes this vision: simple, yet possessing a
unique angular beauty.[4] The early skyscraper, the very
symbol of the Chicago style, represents the triumph of
function and utility over sentiment, America over Europe,
and perhaps even the frontier over the civilization of the

Fig. 2. The Reliance Building. (Photo courtesy of The Art
Institute of Chicago.)

East Coast.[5] These ideals of the original Chicago School were expanded upon by architects of the Second Chicago School. Frank Lloyd Wright's legendary organic style and the famed glass and steel constructions of Mies van der Rohe are often the first images that spring to mind when one thinks of Chicago.

Yet the architecture that is the city's defining attribute is being threatened by the increasing tendency toward development. The root of Chicago's preservation problem lies in the enormous drive toward economic expansion and the potential in Chicago for such growth. The highly competitive market for land in the city means that properties sell for the highest price if the buildings on them can be obliterated to make room for newer, larger developments. Because of this preference on the part of potential buyers, the label "landmark" has become a stigma for property owners. "In other cities, landmark status is sought after — in Chicago, it's avoided at all costs," notes Alan J. Shannon of the *Chicago Tribune.*[6] Even if owners wish to keep their property's original structure, designation as a landmark is still undesirable as it limits the renovations that can be made to a building and thus decreases its value. Essentially, no

Rinder 6

building that has even been recommended for landmark status may be touched without the approval of the Commission on Chicago Historical and Architectural Landmarks, a restriction that considerably diminishes the appeal of the real estate. "We live in a world where the owners say, 'If you judge my property a landmark you are taking money away from me.' And in Chicago the process is stacked in favor of the economics," says former city Planning Commissioner David Mosena.[7]

The Berghoff buildings, which house the Berghoff Restaurant and its facilities, are a prime example of this problem. The restaurant has been a feature of the Loop for more than ninety years. But when the building was proposed for official designation in 1991, the City Council voted against it after considerable urging from the Berghoff family. Neil King, a real estate valuation expert who testified before the Landmark Preservation Committee, stated that "no developer is going to buy this property once it's designated."[8] The LaSalle National Bank told the Berghoffs that it would foreclose on a mortgage for more than $2.7 million if the Council named the Berghoff buildings landmarks.[9] The Berghoff conflict illustrates that the problem of overbearing development cannot be solved simply by assigning landmark status to historic buildings; it is an ongoing struggle between yesterday's creations and today's economic prosperity.

Nowhere is this clash more apparent than on North Michigan Avenue—Chicago's Magnificent Mile. The historic buildings along this block are unquestionably some of the city's finest works. In addition, the Mile is one of Chicago's most prosperous districts, with a massive volume of shoppers traveling there daily. The small-scale, charming buildings envisioned by Arthur Rubloff, the prominent real estate developer who first conceived of the Magnificent Mile in the late 1940s, could not accommodate the crowds. Numerous high-rises, constructed to accommodate the masses that flock to Michigan Avenue, interrupt the cohesion and unity envisioned by the original planners of the Magnificent Mile. In *Chicago's North Michigan Avenue,* John W. Stamper says that with the standard height for new buildings on the avenue currently at about sixty-five stories, the "pleasant shopping promenade" has become a "canyon-like corridor."[10]

Many agree that the individual style of Michigan

Avenue is being lost. In 1995, the same year that the Landmarks Preservation Council of Illinois declared the section of Michigan Avenue from Oak Street to Roosevelt Road one of the state's ten most endangered historic sites, the annual sales of the Magnificent Mile ran around $1 billion and were increasing at an annual rate of about five to seven percent.[11] Clearly, the property's potential as part of a commercial hub is taking priority over its architectural and historic value. The future of this district rests on a precarious balance between Chicago's responsibility for its own heritage and Chicagoans' desire for economic gain. Stamper notes, "What made North Michigan Avenue such an attractive focus of activity in the 1920s is being incrementally destroyed in the interest of maximizing return on the investment."[12]

Perhaps the best single example of the conflict between preservation and development in Chicago is the case of the McCarthy Building (fig. 3). Built in 1872, the McCarthy was designed by John M. Van Osdel, Chicago's first professional architect. Paul Gapp, a *Chicago Tribune* architecture critic, described it as "a stunningly appealing relic from Chicago's 19th century Renaissance era."[13] The McCarthy was made a landmark in 1984, but

Rinder 9

Fig. 3. The McCarthy Building. (From the University of
Illinois at Chicago, *Chicago Imagebase,* http://www.uic.edu/
depts/ahaa/imagebase.)

it wasn't long before developers recognized the potential
of the property, situated on Block 37 of State Street,
directly across from Marshall Field's. With plans for a
$300 million retail and office complex already outlined,
developers made a $12.3 million bid for the property,
promising to preserve the McCarthy and integrate it into
the complex. The city readily agreed. However, a series of
modifications over the next two years completely
transformed the original plan. With the old structure now

useless to the project, developers made subsequent proposals to preserve just the facade, or even to move the entire McCarthy Building to another location. When these propositions didn't work out, the developers began offering to preserve other buildings in exchange for permission to demolish the McCarthy. Gapp admitted that the city was caught in a difficult situation: if it protected the McCarthy, it would be impeding development in an important urban renewal area, and if it allowed demolition, Chicago's landmark protection ordinance would be completely devalued. He nonetheless urged city officials to choose the "long view" and preserve the McCarthy.[14] However, the developers' offer to buy and restore the Reliance Building, at a cost of between $7 million and $11 million, and to contribute $4 million to other preservation efforts, prevailed. In September 1987, the Chicago City Council voted to revoke the McCarthy's landmark status.

Ironically, Chicago's rich architectural heritage may work against its own preservation. With so many significant buildings, losing one does not seem as critical as perhaps it should. The fact that Chicago boasts some forty-five Mies buildings, seventy-five Frank Lloyd

Wright buildings, and numerous other buildings from the first and second Chicago Schools may inspire a nonchalant attitude toward preservation.[15] The public seems to justify the demolition of quality architecture by citing Chicago's vast number of such works. Excusing the razing of Chicago's Arts Club, noted for having the only known interior designed by Mies himself, and other buildings on Michigan Avenue, the city's Planning and Development Commissioner, Valerie Jarrett, told the *Chicago Sun-Times,* "We are a city that is rich in our architectural heritage . . . we do a yeoman's job of preserving those buildings."[16] This rationale is careless; each building is an original creation and should be evaluated as one, not as a faceless member of the group.

The razing of the McCarthy Building in 1987 exposes the problems inherent in Chicago's landmark policy. But the real tragedy is that none of the plans for development of the property were ever carried out. Block 37 remains vacant to this day. Clearly, the city needs creative and vigilant urban planning. Yet some have questioned the importance of such planning, arguing that it stifles innovation and creative advances. Jack Guthman, a Chicago lawyer representing a group of property owners,

Rinder 12

told the *Chicago Tribune* that he opposed landmark designation: "What [those proposing designation are] saying is a clear indictment of today's architecture—that we can't improve on the past."[17] Proponents of this viewpoint, however, neglect one important fact. The city has an extensive history of urban planning, dating back to Burnham's original Chicago Plan of 1909, which posed no hindrance to the likes of Mies and Wright. In addition, just one look at the rapid and disorderly growth of North Michigan Avenue makes it clear that unlimited development is not the answer.

To uphold Chicago's reputation as an architectural jewel, the city must participate in urban planning. The most important municipal duty in managing development is to ease the economic burdens that preservation entails. Some methods that have been suggested for this are property tax breaks for landmark owners and transferable development rights, which would give landmark owners bonuses for developing elsewhere. Overall, however, the city's planning and landmarks commissions simply need to become more involved, working closely with developers throughout the entire design process. If both parties outline their needs,

Rinder 13

restrictions, and priorities and then negotiate until mutually satisfied, a middle ground can be reached. Of course, there are some demands on which the city should not compromise, such as the significance of landmark status. But added cooperation on other fronts could help to mitigate a few strict policies and achieve a practical, productive balance.

The effectiveness of an earnest but open-minded approach to urban planning has already been proven in Chicago. Union Station (fig. 4) is one project that

Fig. 4. Union Station, circa 1925. (Postcard courtesy of Minnie Dangberg.)

Rinder 14

worked to the satisfaction of both developers and preservationists. Developers U.S. Equities Realty Inc. and Amtrak proposed replacing the four floors of outdated office space above the station with more practical high-rise towers. This offer allowed for the preservation of the Great Hall and other public spaces within the station itself. "We are preserving the best of the historical landmark . . . and at the same time creating an adaptive reuse that will bring back some of the old glory of the station," Cheryl Stein of U.S. Equities told the *Tribune*.[18] The city responded to this magnanimous offer in kind, upgrading zoning on the site to permit additional office space and working with developers to identify exactly which portions of the original structure needed to be preserved. Today, the sight of Union Station, revitalized and bustling, is proof of the sincere endeavors of developers and city planners alike.

In the midst of abandonment and demolition, buildings such as Union Station and the Reliance Building offer Chicago some hope for a future that is as architecturally rich as its past. The key to achieving this balance of preserving historic treasures and encouraging new development is to view the city not so much as a

product, but as a process. Robert Bruegmann, author of
The Architects and the City, defines a city as "the
ultimate human artifact, our most complex and
prodigious social creation, and the most tangible result
of the actions over time of all its citizens."[19] Nowhere
is this sentiment more relevant than in Chicago.
Comprehensive urban planning will ensure that the city's
character, so closely tied to its architecture, is preserved.

Notes

1. Tracie Rozhon, "Chicago Girds for Big Battle over Its Skyline," *New York Times,* November 12, 2000, http://www.lexisnexis.com (accessed November 7, 2006).

2. David Garrard Lowe, *Lost Chicago* (New York: Watson-Guptill Publications, 2000), 112.

3. *Microsoft Encarta Encyclopedia 2000,* s.v. "Sullivan, Louis Henri," CD-ROM (Microsoft, 2000).

4. Lowe, *Lost Chicago,* 123.

5. Daniel Bluestone, *Constructing Chicago* (New Haven: Yale University Press, 1991), 105.

6. Alan J. Shannon, "When Will It End?" *Chicago Tribune,* September 11, 1987, quoted in Karen J. Dilibert, *From Landmark to Landfill* (Chicago: Chicago Architectural Foundation, 2000), 11.

7. Steve Kerch, "Landmark Decisions," *Chicago Tribune,* March 18, 1990, sec. 16.

8. Patrick T. Reardon, "'No' Vote Makes It a Landmark Day for the Berghoff," *Chicago Tribune,* April 5, 1991, sec 1.

9. Ibid.

10. John W. Stamper, *Chicago's North Michigan Avenue* (Chicago: University of Chicago Press, 1991), 215.

Rinder 17

11. Nancy Stuenkel, "Success Spoiling the Magnificent Mile?" *Chicago Sun-Times,* April 9, 1995, http://www.lexisnexis.com (accessed November 8, 2006).

12. Stamper, *North Michigan Avenue,* 215.

13. Paul Gapp, "McCarthy Building Puts Landmark Law on a Collision Course with Developers," *Chicago Tribune,* April 20, 1986, quoted in Karen J. Dilibert, *From Landmark to Landfill* (Chicago: Chicago Architectural Foundation, 2000), 4.

14. Ibid.

15. Rozhon, "Chicago Girds for Big Battle."

16. Rich Hein, "Preservationists Rally behind 'Mies and Moe's,'" *Chicago Sun-Times,* November 4, 1994, http://www.lexisnexis.com (accessed November 10, 2006).

17. David Mendell and Gary Washburn, "Daley Acts to Protect Michigan Ave. Skyline," *Chicago Tribune,* March 8, 2001.

18. Kerch, "Landmark Decisions."

19. Robert Bruegmann, *The Architects and the City* (Chicago: University of Chicago Press, 1997), 443.

Rinder 18

Bibliography

Bluestone, Daniel. *Constructing Chicago*. New Haven: Yale
    University Press, 1991.

Bruegmann, Robert. *The Architects and the City*. Chicago:
    University of Chicago Press, 1997.

Dilibert, Karen J. *From Landmark to Landfill*. Chicago:
    Chicago Architectural Foundation, 2000.

Hein, Rich. "Preservationists Rally behind 'Mies and
    Moe's.'" *Chicago Sun-Times,* November 4, 1994. http://
    www.lexisnexis.com (accessed November 10, 2006).

Kerch, Steve. "Landmark Decisions." *Chicago Tribune,*
    March 18, 1990, sec. 16.

Lowe, David Garrard. *Lost Chicago*. New York: Watson-
    Guptill Publications, 2000.

Mendell, David, and Gary Washburn. "Daley Acts to
    Protect Michigan Ave. Skyline." *Chicago Tribune,*
    March 8, 2001.

Reardon, Patrick T. "'No' Vote Makes It a Landmark Day for
    the Berghoff." *Chicago Tribune,* April 5, 1991, sec. 1.

Rozhon, Tracie. "Chicago Girds for Big Battle over Its
    Skyline." *New York Times,* November 12, 2000.
    http://www.lexisnexis.com (accessed November 7,
    2006).

Rinder 19

Stamper, John W. Chicago's *North Michigan Avenue*.
      Chicago: University of Chicago Press, 1991.
Stuenkel, Nancy. "Success Spoiling the Magnificent
      Mile?" *Chicago Sun-Times,* April 9, 1995. http://
      www.lexisnexis.com (accessed November 8, 2006).

6

Research in the Social Sciences

Resources in the Social Sciences

GENERAL REFERENCE SOURCES FOR THE SOCIAL SCIENCES

International Encyclopedia of the Social and Behavioral Sciences. 24 vols., plus two index vols. 2001. Supplies four thousand articles about topics and terms from the major areas in the social and behavioral sciences. (online)

INDEXES AND DATABASES FOR THE SOCIAL SCIENCES

ABI/INFORM. Covers 1971–. Indexes and abstracts academic and popular periodicals. (online)

PAIS International. Covers 1991–. Formerly *PAIS Bulletin*, 1976–1990; *PAIS Foreign Language Index*, 1972–1990; and *Public Affairs Information Service Bulletin*, 1915–1976. Indexes over twelve hundred social science periodicals plus pamphlets, agency reports, government documents, and books on politics, economics, business administration, international relations, and social topics. (online)

Social Sciences Citation Index. Covers 1956–. Indexes citations made in over a thousand social science journals; entries allow tracing influence through the frequency of later citations of books and periodicals. (online via Web of Science)

Social Sciences Full Text. Covers 1974–. Formerly *Social Sciences and Humanities Index,* 1965–1974, and *International Index,* 1907–1965. Indexes and abstracts articles from over three hundred major periodicals on policy sciences, psychology, sociology, social work, gerontology, health, law, criminology, law enforcement, public administration, urban studies, political science, international relations, geography, and many other social science areas. (online)

WEB RESOURCES FOR THE SOCIAL SCIENCES

FedStats: One Stop Shopping for Federal Statistics
www.fedstats.gov
Consolidates access to statistics and data from over seventy federal agencies.

Infomine: Scholarly Internet Resource Collections
infomine.ucr.edu
Supplies indexed and annotated links to databases, government resources, maps, teaching resources, and other materials of academic interest for business, law, geography, and other social sciences.

Intute: Social Sciences
www.intute.ac.uk/socialsciences/lost.html
Facilitates access to thousands of selected resources organized by subject areas or geography.

Open Access Webliography
www.digital-scholarship.com/cwb/oaw.htm
A useful guide to helping scholars find research that is free and not password protected.

Quick Reference
www.lib.utexas.edu/refsites/index.html
Provides access to business and reference resources.

Social Science Data and Databases
www.tntech.edu/history/data.html
Provides links to general social science Web sites.

U.S. Census Bureau
www.census.gov
Supplies demographic, economic, and social data about the U.S. population.

Voice of the Shuttle: Web Page for Humanities Research
vos.ucsb.edu

> Specializes in highlights, top sites, and links to extensive resources in the humanities but also includes anthropology, archaeology, business, law, and political science as well as regional, cultural, media, minority, and gender studies.

Anthropology

GENERAL REFERENCE SOURCES FOR ANTHROPOLOGY

Encyclopedia of Anthropology. 2005. Supplies articles, many illustrated, defining and explaining anthropological terms and topics and including biographical entries. (online)

INDEXES AND DATABASES FOR ANTHROPOLOGY

Abstracts in Anthropology. 1970–. Indexes and abstracts articles from periodicals about physical, linguistic, and cultural anthropology and about archeological sites and artifacts. (online)

Anthropological Literature. 1979–. Indexes articles and essays on anthropology and archaeology, including art history, demography, economics, and religious studies. (online)

WEB RESOURCES FOR ANTHROPOLOGY

Anthro.net
anthro.net

> Allows searches and provides extensive links to reviewed sites and bibliographic references in anthropology and archaeology.

Anthropology in the News
anthropology.tamu.edu/news.htm

> Lists links to current anthropology-related news stories.

Anthropology Resources on the Internet
www.anthropologie.net

> Links to an extensive array of resources on anthropology and archaeology, including academic institutions, museums, and electronic discussion groups.

Anthro TECH: Central On-Line Clearing House for Anthropological Resources and Web Services
www.anthrotech.com
> Supplies images and links to resources in applied, cultural, linguistic, and physical anthropology as well as archaeology.

ArchNet
archnet.asu.edu
> Links to resources and field sites in archaeology, grouped by region, subject, museum, academic institution, and so forth.

Fieldwork: The Anthropologist in the Field
www.ianth.org/fieldwork/tamakoshil
> Creates a "fieldwork experience" including definitions of terms, graphics, and information about the procedures of anthropologists in the field.

The WWW Virtual Library—Anthropology
vlib.anthrotech.com
> Allows keyword searches and provides annotated links to many subfields of anthropology.

Business and Economics

GENERAL REFERENCE SOURCES FOR BUSINESS AND ECONOMICS

Encyclopedia of Banking and Finance. 1994. Includes brief definitions of terms and longer explanations of trends, historical background, government regulations, and related topics. (online)

International Encyclopedia of Business and Management. 6 vols. 2002. Includes five hundred entries covering biographies of important figures and general and country-specific business and management topics.

International Encyclopedia of Economics. 2 vols. 1997. Contains almost four hundred articles that cover topics ranging from monetary theory and international trade to welfare economics and the history of economic thought.

McGraw-Hill Dictionary of Modern Economics. 1994. Defines key terms and supplies bibliographies, tables, and graphs.

The New Palgrave: A Dictionary of Economics. 1998. Supplies thousands of entries, including bibliographies on economic history, methods, philosophy, theories, controversies, and major figures.

Occupational Outlook Handbook. 1949–; biennial. Offers information about more than two hundred occupations, including requirements, conditions, earnings, locations, and projections. (online at http://www.bls.gov/oco)

INDEXES AND DATABASES FOR BUSINESS AND ECONOMICS

Business Index. 1979–. Covers last four years, and indexes more than eight hundred business periodicals and newspapers as well as hundreds of other sources. (online)

Business Periodicals Index. 1958–. Formerly *Industrial Arts Index*, 1913–1957. Indexes and abstracts articles from over 250 business periodicals and newspapers. (online)

Encyclopedia of Business Information Sources. 1988. Lists indexes of periodicals, databases, sources of statistical information, organizations, and other resources available on hundreds of business topics.

Gale Group F&S Index United States Annual. 1972–. Indexes by industry, product, and company name, supplying full text and abstracts from over 750 periodicals on business and financial topics. (online)

International Bibliography of Economics. 1952–. Lists articles, books, and other resources about economics, including history and policy, as well as topics such as money, income, production, and markets.

WEB RESOURCES FOR BUSINESS AND ECONOMICS

The BizTech Network
www.brint.com
Allows searches and provides links to articles, papers, magazines, tools, and many other resources for "contemporary business, management, and information technology issues."

Business and Economics Resources
www.ipl.org/div/subject/browse/bus00.00.00

Alphabetically lists links to many different resources, including sites on careers in the business world.

Business Week Online
www.businessweek.com
Offers online versions of some *Business Week* stories, quick news updates, stock and mutual-fund tracking data, and advertisements—some of which may, in fact, be useful.

Galaxy Business General Resources
www.galaxy.com/directory/44
Links to a variety of resources for business; includes prices, statistics, trends, and general reading sources.

International Business Resources on the WWW
ciber.msu.edu
Specializes in links to international business sites. Also offers keyword searches, browsing, and a variety of other links.

Internet and Marketing
www.ntu.edu.sg/lib/mktg/int-mktg.htm
A site geared to advertising and marketing on the Internet; offers links to statistics, market research, and other resources.

Rutgers Accounting Web
accounting.rutgers.edu
Contains information on and links to all areas of accounting, including searches and resources on finance, taxation, government agencies, and publications.

SEC EDGAR Database
www.sec.gov/edgar.shtml
The Electronic Data Gathering, Analysis, and Retrieval (EDGAR) system is the U.S. Securities and Exchange Commission's archive of business filings. Includes various search capabilities and a wide range of information.

WebEc
www.helsinki.fi/WebEc
An award-winning site that attempts to categorize all the free information on economics available on the Web. Organized by content

area, the site is easily searchable and includes a valuable list of economics journals.

Communications, Journalism, and Linguistics

GENERAL REFERENCE SOURCES FOR COMMUNICATIONS, JOURNALISM, AND LINGUISTICS

Communication Yearbook. 1977–. Includes essays reviewing current topics each year from various viewpoints. (online, e-book)

Encyclopedic Dictionary of Semiotics, Media, and Communications. 2000. Includes entries that define and describe terms, concepts, people, schools of thought, and movements in various disciplines, including semiotics, media and communication studies, anthropology, psychology, and computer science.

International Encyclopedia of Communications. 4 vols. 2003. Supplies extended entries on communications—ancient and modern, verbal and nonverbal—as well as historical and current influences and processes. (online)

International Encyclopedia of Linguistics. 4 vols. 2003. Provides entries, generally with bibliographies, on linguistic terms and topics, languages, language families, and related topics. (online)

Webster's New World Dictionary of Media and Communications. 1996. Supplies brief entries defining terms used in publishing, broadcasting, journalism, film, public relations, and related areas.

INDEXES AND DATABASES FOR COMMUNICATIONS, JOURNALISM, AND LINGUISTICS

Communication Abstracts. 1978–. Indexes and abstracts articles from communication and speech periodicals. (online)

Language and Language Behavior Abstracts (LLBA). 1967–. Provides the definitive index to materials on the nature and use of language. Covers research in linguistics (the nature and structure of human speech), in language (speech sounds, sentence and word structure, meaning in language forms, spelling, phonetics), and in pathologies of speech, language, and hearing. (online)

WEB RESOURCES FOR COMMUNICATIONS, JOURNALISM, AND LINGUISTICS

American Amateur Press Association
members.aol.com/aapa96
>   Provides examples of amateur journalism, tips from professional journalists, and links to resources for writers.

American Communication Association
www.americancomm.org
>   The American Communication Association sponsors this full-coverage site, with links to the subfields in communications organized by field and by interest.

Communication Studies
www.uiowa.edu/~commstud/resources
>   From the University of Iowa, this site offers a wide range of links to listservs, journals, Web research guides, and electronic style guides in fields from advertising to rhetoric.

Investigative Reporters and Editors
www.ire.org
>   An organization dedicated to teaching the skills and issues of investigative journalism; the site's resource center includes a database of more than eleven thousand abstracts of investigative articles.

Linguistic Society of America
www.lsadc.org
>   Provides information on many aspects of linguistics and links to related resources.

Links to Friendly Communications Homepages
www.csufresno.edu/comm/wscalink.htm
>   From the Western States Communication Association, this site provides easy access to many organizational home pages in communications.

News on the Net
www.reporter.org/news

Provides links to numerous news sources, including newspapers, magazines, and television stations.

SIL International
www.sil.org
Offers information about language communities worldwide. Supports research in all areas of linguistics.

The WWW Virtual Library—Journalism
vlib.org/communication
Provides search capability and numerous links to resources on media, broadcasting, communications, and news.

Education

GENERAL REFERENCE SOURCES FOR EDUCATION

Encyclopedia of Education. 2nd ed. 8 vols. 2003. Supplies full articles, especially on historical topics. (online)

Encyclopedia of Educational Research. 4 vols. 1992. Summarizes research studies and includes bibliographies.

Encyclopedia of Physical Education, Fitness, and Sports. 4 vols. 1977–1985, 1991. Includes articles on historical topics, fitness, training, nutrition, exercise, and specific activities and sports.

The International Encyclopedia of Education. 12 vols. 1994. Contains over twelve hundred entries organized alphabetically within twenty-two major categories, including adult education, girls and women in education, policy and planning, and vocational education and training.

International Encyclopedia of Education: Research and Studies. 10 vols. 1985–1992. Supplies full entries on many general and specialized areas of education.

INDEXES AND DATABASES FOR EDUCATION

Current Index to Journals in Education (CIJE). 1969–2001. Indexes and abstracts articles from education periodicals; *Resources in Education* (1966–) abstracts unpublished materials such as reports and curriculum guides. (online via ERIC)

Education: A Guide to Reference and Information Sources. 1989. Guide to books, periodicals, and databases about education. (online)

Education Index. 1929–. Indexes articles from over 350 education periodicals. (online)

ERIC (Educational Resources Information Center). 1966–. Lists more than 1.2 million articles, papers, and reports on education from more than 650 journals. (online at eric.ed.gov)

Physical Education Index. 1978–. Indexes articles on physical education and sports from several hundred periodicals. (online)

WEB RESOURCES FOR EDUCATION

EdWeb: Exploring Technology and School Reform
edwebproject.org/wwwedu.html
Supplies lively information and access to resources on education, educational policy, current reform efforts, and the impact of technological innovation on education.

National Center for Education Statistics (NCES)
nces.ed.gov
Provides access to information about U.S. education, including publications, surveys, and other data on student achievement, current issues, and related topics.

U.S. Department of Education (ED.gov)
www.ed.gov
Includes information on federal education priorities, financial aid, federal programs and funding, publications, research and statistics.

Ethnic Studies

GENERAL REFERENCE SOURCES FOR ETHNIC STUDIES

The African American Almanac. 2003. Discusses African American history and present-day issues, and includes a bibliography, illustrations, lists, and other data.

The American Indian: A Multimedia Encyclopedia. 1995. Supplies history, tribal backgrounds, documents, songs, biographies, maps, and other information about Native Americans. (CD-ROM)

Asian American Almanac. 2004. Explores the culture and history of American descendents of Asian and Pacific Island immigrants.

The Asian American Encyclopedia. 1995. Discusses the history, language, and culture of both large and small groups of Asian Americans—Chinese, Filipinos, Japanese, Indians, Koreans, Vietnamese, Hmong, and Pacific Islanders—and their influences on and experiences in American culture.

Atlas of the North American Indian. 2000. Includes maps, illustrations, and explanatory text on Native American history, culture, migrations, lands, wars, and other topics from ancient to recent times.

Blackwell Companion to Jewish Culture: From the Eighteenth Century to the Present. 1989. Supplies articles on Jewish culture, notable figures, and contributions in the humanities, sciences, and social sciences.

Dictionary of Asian American History. 1986. Provides essays and brief definitions on the history of Asians and Pacific Islanders in the United States, including cultural and social background, major events, and legal history. (online)

Dictionary of Mexican American History. 1981. Includes entries on history, politics, and social topics, including a chronology, a glossary, statistical tables, and maps.

Encyclopedia of Native American Tribes. 2006. Supplies articles, including illustrations, about 150 tribes and general topics. (online)

Encyclopedia of World Cultures. 10 vols. 1991–1996. Supplies entries and bibliographies on all cultural groups.

Handbook of North American Indians. 20 vols. 1900–1988. Provides essays, including bibliographies and illustrations, on many cultural and historical topics.

Harvard Encyclopedia of American Ethnic Groups. 1980-. Contains articles, maps, and tables on 106 ethnic groups, regional groups, and related topics.

The Hispanic-American Almanac. 2003. Discusses Hispanic American history and present-day issues, and includes bibliographies, illustrations, lists, and other materials.

A Native American Encyclopedia: History, Culture, and Peoples. 2000. Provides information on contemporary and historical customs, dress, habitat, weapons, government, and religions of over two hundred North

American Indian groups; organized by geographical area and alphabetically within each area.

Sourcebook of Hispanic Culture in the United States. 1982. Supplies annotated entries on books, periodicals, and other materials about major Hispanic groups.

The State of Black America. 2004. Includes articles on various social, economic, political, legal, and educational topics of current concern, analyzed by the National Urban League.

We the People: An Atlas of America's Ethnic Diversity. 1988. Supplies maps, explanatory text, and bibliographies on the origins and migrations of sixty-six ethnic groups.

INDEXES AND DATABASES FOR ETHNIC STUDIES

Afro-American Reference: An Annotated Bibliography of Selected Sources. 1985. Supplies annotated entries about reference books and research collections on African Americans.

Asian American Studies: An Annotated Bibliography and Research Guide. 1989. Lists books and articles on a range of topics.

Chicano Index. 1989–1992. Formerly *Chicano Periodical Index,* 1967–1988. Indexes resources on Mexican Americans and has recently added other Spanish-speaking groups. (online)

A Comprehensive Bibliography for the Study of American Minorities. 2 vols. 1976. Supplies annotated entries on thirty-seven minority groups.

Ethnic News Watch. Indexes and supplies full articles from over eighty periodicals representing a wide range of ethnic viewpoints. (online)

Guide to Research on North American Indians. 1983. Supplies annotated entries on articles, books, and government materials on a great variety of topics.

Hispanic American Periodicals Index (HAPI). 1970–. Indexes articles from about 250 periodicals treating Hispanic topics in Latin America and the United States. (online)

International Index to Black Periodicals. 1984–. Formerly *Index to Periodical Articles by and about Blacks,* 1971–1983, and *Index to Periodical Articles by and about Negroes,* 1960–1972. Indexes articles from periodicals. (online)

Native Americans: An Annotated Bibliography. 1991. Lists articles and books, including those focused on a single tribe.

Native Americans: Current Issues. 2002. Collected resources on current issues facing Native Americans, such as Indian Law, Indian heritage, and gaming.

Native Americans: Social, Economic, and Political Aspects: A Bibliography. 1998. Popular bibliography of articles and books concerning Native Americans.

Women of Color in the United States: A Guide to the Literature. 1989. Supplies annotated entries on major resources.

WEB RESOURCES FOR ETHNIC STUDIES

Africa Web Links: An Annotated Resource List
www.africa.upenn.edu/Home_Page/WWW_Links.html
> Supplies annotated links, multimedia archives, and other resources on African and black culture, arts, history, and issues.

The African-American Mosaic: A Library of Congress Resource Guide for the Study of Black History and Culture
lcweb.loc.gov/exhibits/african/intro.html
> Samples of information and images from the collections of the Library of Congress on colonization, abolition, migration, and the WPA.

Ancestors in the Americas
www.cetel.org
> Devoted to publishing and producing resources in the area of multiculturalism, with a special emphasis on Asian and Asian American concerns.

CLNet (Chicano-Latino Network)
latino.sscnet.ucla.edu
> Includes links to Chicano and Latino research, curricula, regional information, data, and other information.

The International Institute
www.umich.edu/~iinet/index.html

Includes resources and links to other Web sites for many University of Michigan programs, such as African American and African, Chinese, Japanese, Russian and Eastern European, and other international studies.

LANIC (Latin American Network Information Center)
lanic.utexas.edu

Provides access by country or topic to a great range of cultural, political, historical, economic, statistical, and other information for over twenty-five Latin American countries.

NativeWeb
www.nativeweb.org

Consolidates hundreds of links to resources, data, news, and information about events concerning native and indigenous peoples, organized by subject, country, and region.

The WWW Virtual Library—Asian Studies
coombs.anu.edu.au/WWWVL-AsianStudies.html

Contains a broad range of information and resources, including links to subject-oriented bibliographies on dozens of individual countries.

The WWW Virtual Library—Migration and Ethnic Relations
www.ercomer.org/wwwvl

Provides an Interactive Information Board and links to research sites, academic institutions, publications, and other resources.

Geography

GENERAL REFERENCE SOURCES FOR GEOGRAPHY

Encyclopedia of Geographic Information Sources: U.S. Volume. 1987. Indexes sources by city, state, and area.

Geo-Data: The World Geographical Encyclopedia. 2003. Includes relief maps and descriptions of the physical geography of every country in the world. (online)

World Geographical Encyclopedia. 5 vols. 1995. Contains information on the environments, populations, economies, histories, and cultures of over 190 countries and a general study of geography and world

statistics; arranged in volumes by continent and organized thematically within each volume.

INDEXES AND DATABASES FOR GEOGRAPHY

Geographical Abstracts: Physical Geography. 1989–. Formerly part of *Geological Abstracts: Paleontology and Stratigraphy.* Indexes and abstracts articles from over one thousand periodicals as well as books, papers, and reports on physical geography and cartography, including topics such as landforms, climatology, hydrology, and meteorology. (online)

WEB RESOURCES FOR GEOGRAPHY

Colorado University: Resources for Geographers
www.Colorado.edu/geography/virtdept/resources/contents.htm
Provides resource lists, organized by topic; search engines; and links to journals, newsgroups, organizations, and other geography-related information.

CU Boulder Internet Resources for Geographers
www.colorado.edu/geography/virtdept/resources/contents.htm
Links to references, lists, journals, organizations, libraries, map collections, databases, and other resources in geography.

Geographic Nameserver
sipb-server-1.mit.edu/geo
Supplies information about places, primarily in the United States, including state, county, latitude, longitude, elevation, and population.

Manual of Federal Geographic Data Products: USGS Index
www.brown.edu/Departments/Taubman_Center/databank/fedgis.html
Provides maps, photographs, and reports on topics such as mineral and energy resources, water and flood conditions, and earthquake information, plus links to resources from other federal agencies.

U.S. Gazetteer
www.census.gov/cgi-bin/gazetteer
Searches for locations in the United States, identifying them for viewing through the Tiger Map Server and for finding corresponding census data.

The WWW Virtual Library — Geography
www.icomos.org/WWW_VL_Geography.html
  Organizes linked resources, maps, databases of names, data, and
  other materials by subject, including countries and academic institutions.

Law and Criminal Justice

GENERAL REFERENCE SOURCES FOR LAW AND CRIMINAL JUSTICE

Encyclopedia of Crime and Justice. 4 vols. 2002. Supplies articles, including
  reference lists, on major topics, including differing points of view.
  (online)

Encyclopedia of the American Constitution. 4 vols. 2000. Contains long articles on laws, acts, decisions, notable figures, and historical periods,
  combining legal, historical, and political science viewpoints.
  (online)

*Encyclopedia of the American Judicial System: Studies of the Principal Institutions
  and Processes of Law.* 3 vols. 1987. Supplies essays on legal history,
  processes, and issues.

Guide to American Law: Everyone's Legal Encyclopedia. 12 vols. 1985,
  1990–1995. Supplies definitions and extended articles on legal terms,
  topics, history, theory, and institutions. Includes an extensive appen-
  dix with sample forms, documents, and a time line.

The Oxford Companion to American Law. 2002. Contains 468 alphabetically
  arranged entries comprising biographies, concepts, current legal
  issues, definitions, descriptions of law enforcement agents and institutions (such as detectives and the FBI) and summaries of cases.
  (online)

INDEXES AND DATABASES FOR LAW AND CRIMINAL JUSTICE

Current Law Index. 1980–. Indexes hundreds of law periodicals. (online)

Index to Legal Periodicals. 1908–. Indexes articles from over four hundred
  law periodicals. (online)

WEB RESOURCES FOR LAW AND CRIMINAL JUSTICE

ASIL Guide to Electronic Resources for International Law
www.asil.org/resource/Home.htm
> Sponsored by the American Society of International Law, this site provides advice on research and extensive links to all major areas of international law.

Cornell Law School Legal Information Institute
www.law.cornell.edu
> "The Legal Information Institute is a research and electronic publishing activity of the Cornell Law School. Popular collections include: the U.S. Code, Supreme Court opinions," and Wex, a free legal dictionary and encyclopedia.

FindLaw
www.findlaw.com
> Legal resources organized by subject: accidents and injuries, bankruptcy and debt, and so on.

HeinOnline
heinonline.org
> Fully searchable legal database with content going back over four centuries.

Hieros Gamos Worldwide Legal Dictionaries
www.hg.org
> Link library specializing in foreign and international law.

Internet Legal Resource Guide
www.ilrg.com
> An extensive index, by category, of selected Web sites and files; designed for laypersons as well as legal scholars.

Law Library Research Exchange (LLRX)
www.llrx.com/sources.html
> An award-winning search engine; provides up-to-date information and extensive links to a broad range of legal research and issues.

National Criminal Justice Reference Service
www.ncjrs.org
> Provides extensive information, statistics, and reports about criminal justice, crime prevention, courts, law enforcement, and related topics, with links to federal agencies, offices, and databases.

Pace Law Library
http://library.law.pace.edu/research/flt.html
> A service of Pace University, this site contains a great list of resources on feminist law, ranging from scholarly journals, to Web links, to institutions that address key feminist legal issues.

U.S. Department of Justice
www.usdoj.gov
> Supplies links to Department of Justice divisions, offices, and programs, as well as links to other federal and criminal justice sites.

WestLaw
westlaw.com
> Westlaw is an online legal research service providing access to legal resources, news articles, and business information.

The WWW Virtual Library—Law
www.law.indiana.edu/v-lib
> Presents an extensive array of sites and resources, organized by legal specialty and topic, as well as by law school, legal firm, journal, government agency, and so on.

Political Science

GENERAL REFERENCE SOURCES FOR POLITICAL SCIENCE

Almanac of American Politics: The President, the Senators, the Representatives, the Governors: Their Records and Election Results, Their States and Districts. 1972–. Biennial. Analyzes state and national politics, including data and maps. (online)

Congressional Quarterly. 1945–. Analyzes national politics, including congressional legislation and voting records, presidential speeches, and Supreme Court decisions. (online)

Political Handbook of the World. 1927–. Supplies current political information about individual countries and their connections through intergovernmental bodies.

State Legislative Sourcebook: A Resource Guide to Legislative Information in the 50 States. 1986–; annual. Lists publications and telephone numbers for state legislatures.

INDEXES AND DATABASES FOR POLITICAL SCIENCE

Political Science: A Guide to Reference and Information Sources. 1990. Supplies annotated entries on political science sources, including databases, research collections, and organizations.

Population Index. 1935–. Ceased in print 1999. Supplies abstracts of periodical articles and other resources dealing with population theories, studies, research methods, statistics, and changes in patterns of birth, migration, and death. (Available online at jstor.org/journals, or popindex.princeton.edu.)

United States Political Science Documents. 1975–. Ceased in print 1991. Indexes scholarly periodicals in political science. (online)

Worldwide Political Science Abstracts. Formerly *ABC Pol Sci: A Bibliography of Current Contents: Political Science and Government.* 1969–2000. Supplies tables of contents from several hundred periodicals in political science, government, economics, law, and sociology.

WEB RESOURCES FOR POLITICAL SCIENCE

Democratic Party Online
www.democrats.org
    The home page of the Democratic National Committee, with useful links to party news, issues, and initiatives.

DTIC
www.dtic.mil
    The Defense Technical Information Center is the U.S. military's own information service, with very detailed coverage of the Defense Technical Information Web and links to specific databases.

Fedworld
www.fedworld.gov
    Links to government services and databases. Provides good search facilities and explanations, with information on how to order materials.

The Gallup Organization
www.gallup.com
    Allows searches and includes up-to-date information and links to a variety of polling-related news items.

Political Resources on the Net
www.politicalresources.net
> Contains political sites, organized by country, with links to parties, governments, organizations, and other political resources; allows searches.

Political Science Resources on the Web
www.lib.umich.edu/govdocs/polisci.html
> Provides extensive annotated links and searches to many political sites and publications.

Political Science Virtual Library
lib.uconn.edu/PoliSci/polisci.htm
> Links to departments, libraries, journals, government agencies, newsgroups, and listservs in related fields.

Republican Main Street
www.rnc.org
> The home page of the Republican National Committee, with many useful links, not all to party issues.

Thomas: Legislative Information on the Internet
thomas.loc.gov
> A site for current and historical federal legislation resources from the Library of Congress, with searches and links to current legislation, *Congressional Record* archives, historical documents, and other government resources.

United Nations
www.un.org
> A good general site, with links to many UN offices, policies, and activities. Also available in French and Spanish.

The White House
www.whitehouse.gov
> The presidential site, with links to the president and vice president, commonly requested federal services, news, a virtual library, and other executive-branch links.

Psychology

GENERAL REFERENCE SOURCES FOR PSYCHOLOGY

The Corsini Encyclopedia of Psychology and Behavioral Science. 4 vols. 2002. Provides over twelve hundred entries covering biographical information on important figures, the history of psychology, psychological theory, and concepts and techniques in areas such as applied, cognitive, educational, physiological, and social psychology. (online)

Encyclopedia of Psychology. 8 vols. 2000. Supplies articles, along with reference lists, on many topics in psychology, including biographies of notable figures.

Oxford Companion to the Mind. 2004. Provides definitions and articles on topics and major figures in psychology, and includes other approaches to the mind as varied as the computer sciences, the fine arts, medicine, and traditional myths. (online)

INDEXES AND DATABASES FOR PSYCHOLOGY

Bibliographic Guide to Psychology. 1974–2003. Comprehensively lists materials in all areas of psychology.

Mental Health Abstracts. 1969–. Formerly *NIMH Data Base.* Abstracts articles from over a thousand journals, as well as books and papers about mental health. (online)

Psychological Abstracts. 1927–. Indexes and abstracts articles from over fourteen hundred psychology periodicals, on many special topics such as developmental, educational, experimental, and social psychology. (online by subscription via PsycINFO)

WEB RESOURCES FOR PSYCHOLOGY

American Psychological Association
www.apa.org
> The APA home page, with access to an online documents search tool, and information for students in psychology.

American Psychological Society
www.psychologicalscience.org
> Links to journals, departments, Net resources and discussion groups, and research information.

Behavior Analysis Resources
www.coedu.usf.edu/behavior/bares.htm
> Links to resources in behavioral psychology.

Freudnet: The Brill Library
www.psychoanalysis.org
> Includes psychoanalytic news, services, and links to electronic research.

Galaxy Psychology Page
galaxy.com/directory/15752/psychology.htm
> A large site divided into clinical, developmental, educational, experimental, and other lists. Also offers a search facility with links to academic organizations, collections, directories, and discussion groups.

Internet Mental Health
www.mentalhealth.com
> Links to the most common mental disorders and medications, news, diagnosis, and help.

Neuropsychology Central
www.neuropsychologycentral.com
> Links to almost any aspect of neuropsychology.

PsychWeb
www.psywww.com
> Contains helpful information and numerous links to psychology resources; geared to students and teachers.

Social Psychology Network
www.socialpsychology.org
> The largest social-psychology database on the Internet; has search capability and links to more than five thousand resources.

The Virtual Psychology Library
www.dialogical.net/psychology
> Good general links to major international psychology sites.

Sociology and Social Work

GENERAL REFERENCE SOURCES FOR SOCIOLOGY AND SOCIAL WORK

Encyclopedia of Social Work. 3 vols. 1995. Supplies articles on social work, covering current issues such as adolescent behavior, divorce, homelessness, immigration, and welfare.

International Encyclopedia of Sociology. 2 vols. 1996. Contains 335 entries that illustrate the main topics and concerns in the field of sociology.

INDEXES AND DATABASES FOR SOCIOLOGY AND SOCIAL WORK

Social Work Abstracts. 1994–. Formerly *Social Work Research and Abstracts.* 1977–1993. Indexes and abstracts resources related to social work. (online)

Sociological Abstracts. 1952–. Indexes and abstracts articles, books, papers, and other resources on diverse topics, including the history, methods, and perspectives of the major fields in sociology. (online)

WEB RESOURCES FOR SOCIOLOGY AND SOCIAL WORK

Annual Reviews of Sociology Online
www.annurev.org
Allows searches of databases for downloadable abstracts.

Social Work and Social Services Web Sites
gwbweb.wustl.edu/websites.html
Provides information on abuse and violence, addiction, alternative medicine, emotional support, gender issues, and welfare.

A Sociological Tour through Cyberspace
www.trinity.edu/~mkearl/index.html
Provides links within sociology, including theory, data, methods, paper-writing guides, and inquiry help.

SocioSite
www.sociosite.net/index.php
A social science information system; allows searches and research in any sociological subject.

The SocioWeb
www.socioweb.com
A general site of links and resources, including searches by topic.

The WWW Virtual Library—Sociology
socserv.mcmaster.ca/w3virtsoclib
Links to sites covering research centers, discussion groups, e-journals, organizations, and university departments.

Women's Studies

GENERAL REFERENCE SOURCES FOR WOMEN'S STUDIES

Women's Studies Encyclopedia. 3 vols. 1999. Supplies articles on studies of women from the viewpoints of the natural sciences, the humanities, and the social sciences, including both historical background and recent research. (online)

INDEXES AND DATABASES FOR WOMEN'S STUDIES

G.K. Hall Women's Studies Index. 1989–2002. Ceased in print. Indexes over one hundred periodicals in the field, including popular publications. (online)

Introduction to Library Research in Women's Studies. 1998. Supplies annotated source lists and guidance about research in this area.

Women Studies Abstracts. 1972–. Indexes and abstracts articles from about three hundred periodicals, on topics such as education, employment, family, history, and sex roles. (online by subscription as part of Women's Studies International)

WEB RESOURCES FOR WOMEN'S STUDIES

The American Studies Web
www.georgetown.edu/crossroads/asw
>   Includes links to research sources for women's studies, among other topics in American studies.

International Gay and Lesbian Review
gaybookreviews.info
>   Provides abstracts and reviews of many books related to lesbian, gay, bisexual, and transgender studies.

Internet Gateway: Feminist Majority Foundation
www.feminist.org/gateway
>   Supplies links to selected Internet resources on women and women's issues.

Literary Resources—Feminism and Women's Literature
newark.rutgers.edu/~jlynch/Lit/women.html
  Devoted entirely to women writers and feminist criticism.

The Women's Resource Project!
www.ibiblio.org/cheryb/women/wshome.html
  Provides links to academic programs in women's studies, other sites
  on a range of topics, and library resources.

Women's Studies Resources
www.mith2.umd.edu/WomensStudies
  Includes images, government documents, bibliographies, and other
  resources, as well as links to other sites and library collections.

APA Style

Many fields in the social sciences ask students to follow the basic
guidelines prescribed by the American Psychological Association
(APA) for formatting manuscripts and documenting various kinds of
sources.

For further reference on APA style, consult the *Publication Manual
of the American Psychological Association*, Fifth Edition (2001).

DIRECTORY TO APA STYLE FOR IN-TEXT CITATIONS

1. Author named in a signal phrase, *194*
2. Author named in a parenthetical reference, *195*
3. Two authors, *195*
4. Three to five authors, *195*
5. Six or more authors, *196*
6. Corporate or group author, *196*
7. Unknown author, *196*
8. Two or more authors with the same last name, *196*
9. Two or more works by an author in a single year, *196*
10. Two or more sources in one parenthetical reference, *197*
11. Specific parts of a source, *197*
12. Email and other personal communication, *197*
13. Electronic document, *197*

APA Format for In-Text Citations

APA style requires parenthetical references in the text to document quotations, paraphrases, summaries, and other material from a source. These citations include the year of publication and correspond to full bibliographic entries in the list of references at the end of the text.

1. AUTHOR NAMED IN A SIGNAL PHRASE

In most instances, use the author's name in a signal phrase to introduce the cited material, and place the date, in parentheses, immediately after the author's name. For a quotation, the page number, preceded by *p.,* appears in parentheses after the quotation.

> As Fanderclai (2001) observed, older siblings play an important role in the development of language and learning skills.

> Chavez (2003) noted that "six years after slim cigarettes for women were introduced, more than twice as many teenage girls were smoking" (p. 13).

For electronic texts or other works with paragraph numbers but no page numbers, use the paragraph number preceded by the ¶ symbol or the abbreviation *para.*

> Weinberg (2000) has claimed that "the techniques used in group therapy can be verbal, expressive, or psychodramatic" (¶ 5).

If paragraph numbers are not given, cite the heading and number of the paragraph in that section, if any: *(Types of Groups section, para. 1)*. For a long, set-off quotation (one having more than forty words), place the page reference in parentheses one space after the final punctuation.

2. AUTHOR NAMED IN A PARENTHETICAL REFERENCE

When you do not mention the author in a signal phrase in your text, give the author's name and the date, separated by a comma, in parentheses at the end of the cited material.

One study found that 17% of adopted children in the United States are of a different race than their adoptive parents (Peterson, 2003).

3. TWO AUTHORS

Use both names in all citations. Join the names with *and* in a signal phrase, but use an ampersand (&) instead in a parenthetical reference.

Babcock and Laschever (2003) have suggested that many women do not negotiate their salaries and pay raises as vigorously as their male counterparts do.

A recent study has suggested that many women do not negotiate their salaries and pay raises as vigorously as their male counterparts do (Babcock & Laschever, 2003).

4. THREE TO FIVE AUTHORS

List all the authors' names for the first reference.

Safer, Voccola, Hurd, and Goodwin (2003) reached somewhat different conclusions by designing a study that was less dependent on subjective judgment than were previous studies.

In subsequent references, use just the first author's name plus *et al.* ("and others").

Based on the results, Safer et al. (2003) determined that the apes took significant steps toward self-expression.

5. SIX OR MORE AUTHORS

Use only the first author's name and *et al.* ("and others") in every citation, including the first.

As Soleim et al. (2002) demonstrated, advertising holds the potential for manipulating "free-willed" consumers.

6. CORPORATE OR GROUP AUTHOR

If the name of the organization or corporation is long, spell it out the first time you use it, followed by an abbreviation in brackets. In later references, use the abbreviation only.

FIRST CITATION   (Centers for Disease Control and Prevention [CDC], 2006)
LATER CITATIONS (CDC, 2006)

7. UNKNOWN AUTHOR

Use the title or its first few words in a signal phrase or in parentheses. Italicize a book or report title; place an article title in quotation marks.

The school profiles for the county substantiate this trend (*Guide to secondary schools, 2003*).

8. TWO OR MORE AUTHORS WITH THE SAME LAST NAME

If your list of references includes works by different authors with the same last name, include the authors' initials in each citation.

G. Jones (2001) conducted the groundbreaking study on teenage childbearing.

9. TWO OR MORE WORKS BY AN AUTHOR IN A SINGLE YEAR

Assign lowercase letters (*a*, *b*, and so on) alphabetically by title, and include the letters after the year.

Gordon (2004b) examined this trend in more detail.

10. TWO OR MORE SOURCES IN ONE PARENTHETICAL REFERENCE

List sources by different authors in alphabetical order by authors' last names, separated by semicolons; list works by the same author in chronological order, separated by commas.

(Cardone, 2004; Lai, 2002)

(Lai, 2000, 2002)

11. SPECIFIC PARTS OF A SOURCE

Use abbreviations (*chap., p., para.,* and so on) in a parenthetical reference to name the part of a work you are citing.

Mogolov (2003, chap. 9) has argued that his research yielded
the opposite results.

12. EMAIL AND OTHER PERSONAL COMMUNICATION

Cite any personal letters, email messages, electronic postings, telephone conversations, or interviews with the person's initial(s) and last name, the identification *personal communication,* and the date. Do not include personal communications in the reference list.

R. Tobin (personal communication, November 4, 2005)
supported his claims about music therapy with new evidence.

13. ELECTRONIC DOCUMENT

To cite an entire Web site, include its address in parentheses in your text (http://www.gallup.com); you do not need to include it in your list of references. Otherwise, cite a Web or electronic document as you would a print source, using the author's name and date; indicating the chapter or figure, as appropriate; and giving a full citation in your list of references. To cite a quotation, include the page or paragraph numbers.

In her report, Zomkowski stressed the importance of "ensuring equitable access to the Internet" (2003, para. 3).

APA Format for Content Notes

APA style allows you to use content notes to expand or supplement your text. Indicate such notes in the text by superscript numerals ([1]). Type the notes themselves on a separate page after the last page of the text, under the heading *Footnotes,* which should be centered at the top of the page. Double-space all entries. Indent the first line of each note one-half inch (or five to seven spaces), but begin subsequent lines at the left margin.

SUPERSCRIPT NUMBER IN TEXT

The age of the children involved in the study was an important factor in the selection of items for the questionnaire.[1]

FOOTNOTE

[1]Marjorie Youngston Forman and William Cole of the Child Study Team provided great assistance in identifying appropriate items for the questionnaire.

APA Format for a List of References

The alphabetical list of the sources cited in your document is called *References.* (If your instructor asks that you list everything you have read as background — not just the sources you cite — call the list *Bibliography.*) Here are guidelines for preparing a list of references:

- Start your list on a separate page after the text of your document but before any appendices or notes. Identify each page with the short title and page number, continuing the numbering of the text.

- Type the heading *References,* neither italicized nor in quotation marks, centered one inch from the top of the page.

- Double-space, and begin your first entry. Unless your instructor suggests otherwise, do not indent the first line of each entry, but indent subsequent lines one-half inch or five to seven spaces. Double-space the entire list.

- List sources alphabetically by authors' (or editors') last names. If the author is unknown, alphabetize the source by the first major word of the title, disregarding *A, An,* or *The.* If the list includes two or more works by the same author, see the examples on pp. 203 and 207.

APA style specifies the treatment and placement of four basic elements — author, publication date, title, and other publication information.

- *Author.* List all authors' last names first, and use only initials for first and middle names. Separate the names of multiple authors with commas, and use an ampersand (&) before the last author's name.

- *Publication date.* Enclose the date in parentheses. Use only the year for books and journals; use the year, a comma, and the month or month and day for magazines; use the year, a comma, and the month and day for newspapers. Do not abbreviate.

- *Title.* Italicize titles and subtitles of books and periodicals. Do not enclose titles of articles in quotation marks. For books and articles, capitalize only the first word of the title and subtitle and any proper nouns or proper adjectives. Capitalize all major words in a periodical title.

- *Publication information.* For a book, list the city of publication (and the country or postal abbreviation for the state if the city is unfamiliar), a colon, and the publisher's name, dropping any *Inc., Co.,* or *Publishers.* For a periodical, follow the periodical title with a comma, the volume number (italicized), the issue number (if appropriate) in parentheses and followed by a comma, and the inclusive page numbers of the article. For newspaper articles and for articles or chapters in books, include the abbreviation *p.* ("page") or *pp.* ("pages") before the page numbers.

The sample entries that start on p. 201 use a hanging indent format, in which the first line aligns on the left and the subsequent lines indent one-half inch or five to seven spaces. This is the customary APA format for final copy, including student papers.

DIRECTORY TO APA STYLE FOR REFERENCES

BOOKS

1. One author, *201*
2. Two or more authors, *201*
3. Corporate or group author, *201*
4. Unknown author, *202*
5. Editor, *202*
6. Selection in a book with an editor, *202*
7. Translation, *202*
8. Edition other than the first, *202*
9. Multivolume work, *202*
10. Article in a reference work, *203*
11. Republication, *203*
12. Two or more works by the same author(s), *203*

PERIODICALS

13. Article in a journal paginated by volume, *203*
14. Article in a journal paginated by issue, *206*
15. Article in a magazine, *206*
16. Article in a newspaper, *206*
17. Editorial or letter to the editor, *206*
18. Unsigned article, *206*
19. Review, *206*
20. Published interview, *206*
21. Two or more works by the same author in the same year, *207*

ELECTRONIC SOURCES

22. Article in an online periodical, *208*
23. Article or abstract from a database, *208*
24. Document from a Web site, *209*
25. Chapter or section of a Web document, *209*
26. Email message or real-time communication, *209*
27. Online posting, *212*
28. Software or computer program, *212*

(Continued)

Books

The basic format for a reference-list entry for a book is outlined on pp. 204–5.

1. ONE AUTHOR

Lightman, A. P. (2002). *The diagnosis.* New York: Vintage Books.

2. TWO OR MORE AUTHORS

Walsh, M. E., & Murphy, J. A. (2003). *Children, health, and learning: A guide to the issues.* Westport, CT: Praeger.

3. CORPORATE OR GROUP AUTHOR

Committee on Abrupt Climate Change, National Research Council. (2002). *Abrupt climate change: Inevitable surprises.* Washington, DC: National Academies Press.

Use the word *Author* as the publisher when the organization is both the author and the publisher.

Resources for Rehabilitation. (2003). *A woman's guide to coping with disability.* London: Author.

4. UNKNOWN AUTHOR

National Geographic atlas of the Middle East. (2003). Washington, DC: National Geographic Society.

5. EDITOR

Dickens, J. (Ed.). (1995). *Family outing: A guide for parents of gays, lesbians, and bisexuals.* London: Peter Owen.

6. SELECTION IN A BOOK WITH AN EDITOR

Burke, W. W., & Nourmair, D. A. (2001). The role of personality assessment in organization development. In J. Waclawski & A. H. Church (Eds.), *Organization development: A data-driven approach to organizational change* (pp. 55–77). San Francisco: Jossey-Bass.

7. TRANSLATION

Al-Farabi, A. N. (1998). *On the perfect state* (R. Walzer, Trans.). Chicago: Kazi.

8. EDITION OTHER THAN THE FIRST

Moore, G. S. (2002). *Living with the earth: Concepts in environmental health science* (2nd ed.). New York: Lewis.

9. MULTIVOLUME WORK

Barnes, J. (Ed.). (1995). *Complete works of Aristotle* (Vols. 1–2). Princeton, NJ: Princeton University Press.

10. ARTICLE IN A REFERENCE WORK

If no author is listed, begin with the title.

Dean, C. (1994). Jaws and teeth. In *The Cambridge encyclopedia of human evolution* (pp. 56 – 59). Cambridge, England: Cambridge University Press.

11. REPUBLICATION

Piaget, J. (1952). *The language and thought of the child.* London: Routledge & Kegan Paul. (Original work published 1932)

12. TWO OR MORE WORKS BY THE SAME AUTHOR(S)

List two or more works by the same author in chronological order (if the works appear in a single year, see model 21). Repeat the author's name in each entry.

Goodall, J. (1999). *Reason for hope: A spiritual journey.* New York: Warner Books.

Goodall, J. (2002). *Performance and evolution in the age of Darwin: Out of the natural order.* New York: Routledge.

Periodicals

The basic format for a reference-list entry for an article in a periodical is outlined on pp. 210–11.

13. ARTICLE IN A JOURNAL PAGINATED BY VOLUME

O'Connell, D. C., & Kowal, S. (2003). Psycholinguistics: A half century of monologism. *The American Journal of Psychology, 116,* 191–212.

SOURCE MAP: Citing books using APA style

Take information from the book's title page and copyright page (on the reverse side of the title page), not from the book's cover or a library catalog.

(1) *Author.* List all authors' last names first, and use only initials for first and middle names. Separate the names of multiple authors with commas, and use an ampersand (&) before the last author's name.

(2) *Publication year.* Enclose the year of publication in parentheses.

(3) *Title.* Italicize the title and subtitle. Capitalize only the first word of the title and the subtitle and any proper nouns or proper adjectives.

(4) *City of publication.* List the city of publication (and the country or state abbreviation if the city is unfamiliar) followed by a colon.

(5) *Publisher.* Give the publisher's name, dropping any *Inc., Co.,* or *Publishers.*

For a book by one author, use the following format:

Last name, initial(s). (Year). *Title of book: Subtitle.* City: Publisher.

A citation for the book on p. 205 would look like this:

AUTHOR'S LAST NAME   YEAR OF   TITLE AND SUBTITLE,
AND INITIAL   PUBLICATION   ITALICIZED

Tsutsui, W. (2004). *Godzilla on my mind: Fifty years of the king of monsters.*

                                 — PUBLISHER'S CITY AND NAME

  → New York: Palgrave Macmillan.

    — DOUBLE-SPACE; INDENT ONE-HALF INCH OR FIVE TO SEVEN SPACES

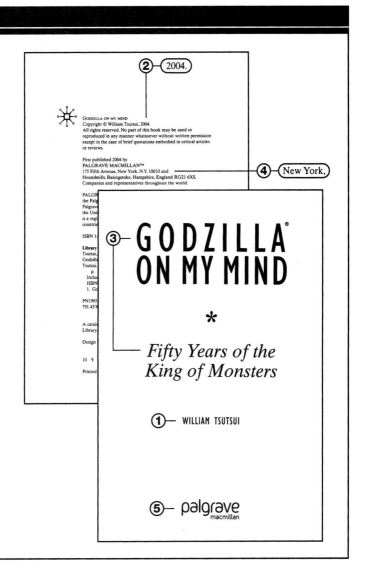

GODZILLA ON MY MIND
Copyright © William Tsutsui, 2004.
All rights reserved. No part of this book may be used or
reproduced in any manner whatsoever without written permission
except in the case of brief quotations embodied in critical articles
or reviews.

First published 2004 by
PALGRAVE MACMILLAN™
175 Fifth Avenue, New York, N.Y. 10010 and
Houndmills, Basingstoke, Hampshire, England RG21 6XS.
Companies and representatives throughout the world.

② — 2004.

④ — New York,

③ — # GODZILLA®
ON MY MIND

*

*Fifty Years of the
King of Monsters*

① — WILLIAM TSUTSUI

⑤ — palgrave
macmillan

14. ARTICLE IN A JOURNAL PAGINATED BY ISSUE

Hall, R. E. (2000). Marriage as vehicle of racism among women of color. *Psychology: A Journal of Human Behavior, 37*(2), 29–40.

15. ARTICLE IN A MAGAZINE

Ricciardi, S. (2003, August 5). Enabling the mobile work force. *PC Magazine, 22,* 46.

16. ARTICLE IN A NEWSPAPER

Faler, B. (2003, August 29). Primary colors: Race and fundraising. *The Washington Post,* p. A5.

17. EDITORIAL OR LETTER TO THE EDITOR

Zelneck, B. (2003, July 18). Serving the public at public universities [Letter to the editor]. *The Chronicle Review,* p. B18.

18. UNSIGNED ARTICLE

Annual meeting announcement. (2003, March). *Cognitive Psychology, 46,* 227.

19. REVIEW

Ringel, S. (2003). [Review of the book *Multiculturalism and the therapeutic process*]. *Clinical Social Work Journal, 31,* 212–213.

20. PUBLISHED INTERVIEW

Smith, H. (2002, October). [Interview with A. Thompson]. *The Sun,* pp. 4–7.

21. TWO OR MORE WORKS BY THE SAME AUTHOR
IN THE SAME YEAR

List the works alphabetically by title, and place lowercase letters (*a, b,* etc.) after the dates.

Shermer, M. (2002a). On estimating the lifetime of civilizations. *Scientific American, 287*(2), 33.

Shermer, M. (2002b). Readers who question evolution. *Scientific American, 287*(1), 37.

Electronic Sources

The *Publication Manual of the American Psychological Association,* Fifth Edition, includes guidelines for citing various kinds of electronic resources, including Web sites; articles, reports, and abstracts; some types of online communications; and computer software. Updated guidelines are maintained at the APA's Web site (www.apa.org).

The basic entry for most sources accessed via the Internet should include the following elements:

- *Author.* Give the author's name, if available.
- *Publication date.* Include the date of electronic publication or of the latest update, if available. Use *n.d.* ("no date") when the publication date is unavailable.
- *Title.* List the title of the document or subject line of the message, neither italicized nor in quotation marks.
- *Publication information.* For articles from online journals, newspapers, or reference databases, give the publication title and other publishing information as you would for a print periodical.
- *Retrieval information.* For most Internet sources, type the word *Retrieved* followed by the date of access, a comma, and the word *from.* End with the URL or other retrieval information and no period. If the URL will not fit on one line, break it after a slash or before a period and do not add a hyphen. For listserv or newsgroup messages and other online postings, type *Message posted to,* followed by the name of the list or group and the URL of the group or its archive.

22. ARTICLE IN AN ONLINE PERIODICAL

If the article also appears in a print journal, no retrieval state-ment is required; instead, include the label *[Electronic version]* after the article title.

> Steedman, M., & Jones, G. P. (2000). Information structure and the syntax-phonology interface [Electronic version]. *Linguistic Inquiry, 31,* 649–689.

However, if the online article differs from the print version (for ex-ample, if page numbers are not indicated) or did not appear in print, include the date of access and the URL.

> Lou, L., & Chen, J. (2003, January). Attention and blind-spot phenomenology. *Psyche, 9*(2). Retrieved March 22, 2003, from http://psyche.cs.monash.edu.au/v9/psyche-9-02-lou .html

23. ARTICLE OR ABSTRACT FROM A DATABASE

(See pp. 214–15 for the basic format for citing an article from a database.) Give the information as you would for a print document. List the date you retrieved the article and the name of the database. If you are citing an abstract, use the notation *Abstract retrieved.* End with the document number in parentheses, if appropriate.

> Crook, S. (2003). Change, uncertainty and the future of sociology. *Journal of Sociology, 39*(1), 7–14. Retrieved January 10, 2004, from Expanded Academic ASAP database (A101260213).

> Hayhoe, G. (2001). The long and winding road: Technology's future. *Technical Communication, 48*(2), 133–145. Retrieved September 22, 2001, from ProQuest database.

McCall, R. B. (1998). Science and the press: Like oil and water?
    American Psychologist, 43(2), 87–94. Abstract retrieved
    August 23, 2002, from PsycINFO database (1988-18263-001).

24. DOCUMENT FROM A WEB SITE

(See pp. 216–17 for the basic format for citing a work from a
Web site.) Include information as you would for a print document,
followed by information about its retrieval. If no author is identified,
give the title of the document followed by the date (if available).

DotComSense: Commonsense ways to protect your privacy and
    assess online mental health information. (2000, January).
    APA Monitor, 31, 32. Retrieved January 25, 2001, from http://
    helping.apa.org/dotcomsense/

To site an entire Web site, give its address in a parenthetical reference
but do not include it in your list of references.

25. CHAPTER OR SECTION OF A WEB DOCUMENT

After the chapter or section title, type *In* and give the document
title, with identifying information, if any, in parentheses. End with
the date of access and the URL.

Salamon, Andrew. (n.d.). War in Europe. In *Childhood in times of war*
    (chap. 2). Retrieved April 11, 2005, from http://remember.org/
    jean

26. EMAIL MESSAGE OR REAL-TIME COMMUNICATION

Do not include entries for email messages or real-time communications (such as IMs) in the list of references; instead, cite these
sources in your text as forms of personal communication (see in-text
model 12 on p. 197).

SOURCE MAP: Citing articles from periodicals using APA style

(1) *Author.* List all authors' last names first, and use only initials for first and middle names. Separate the names of multiple authors with commas, and use an ampersand (&) before the last author's name.

(2) *Publication date.* Enclose the date in parentheses. For journals, use only the year. For magazines and newspapers, use the year, a comma, the month (spelled out), and the day of the month if given.

(3) *Article title.* Do not italicize or enclose article titles in quotation marks. Capitalize only the first word of the article title and subtitle and any proper nouns or proper adjectives.

(4) *Periodical title.* Italicize the periodical title (and subtitle, if any), and capitalize all major words.

(5) *Publication information.* Follow the periodical title with a comma, and then give the volume number (italicized) and, without a space in between, the issue number (if given) in parentheses.

(6) *Page numbers.* Give the inclusive page numbers of the article. For newspapers only, include the abbreviation *p.* ("page") or *pp.* ("pages") before the page numbers. End the citation with a period.

For a basic periodical article, use the following format:

Last name, First initial. (Year, month day [or year alone for journal]). Title of article. *Title of Periodical, Volume number* (Issue number), Page number(s).

A citation for the magazine article on p. 211 would look like this:

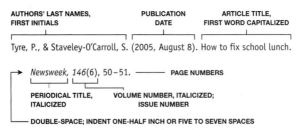

AUTHORS' LAST NAMES, FIRST INITIALS   PUBLICATION DATE   ARTICLE TITLE, FIRST WORD CAPITALIZED

Tyre, P., & Staveley-O'Carroll, S. (2005, August 8). How to fix school lunch.

Newsweek, 146(6), 50–51. ——— PAGE NUMBERS

PERIODICAL TITLE, ITALICIZED   VOLUME NUMBER, ITALICIZED; ISSUE NUMBER

DOUBLE-SPACE; INDENT ONE-HALF INCH OR FIVE TO SEVEN SPACES

① BY PEG TYRE AND
SARAH STAVELEY-O'CARROLL

③ How to Fix School Lunch

Celebrity chefs, politicians and concerned parents are
joining forces to improve the meals kids eat every day.

② AUGUST 8, 2005

④ NEWSWEEK

⑤ Volume CXLVI,

⑥ 50

27. ONLINE POSTING

List an online posting in the references list only if the message is retrievable from a mailing list's archive. Give the author's name and the posting's date and subject line. Include other identifying information in square brackets. For a listserv message, include both the name of the list and the URL of the archived message.

Troike, R. C. (2001, June 21). Buttercups and primroses [Msg 8]. Message posted to the American Dialect Society's electronic mailing list, archived at http://listserv.linguistlist.org/archives/ads-l.html

For a newsgroup posting, end with the name of the news-group. (If the author's real name is unavailable, include the screen name.)

Wittenberg, E. (2001, July 11). Gender and the Internet [Msg 4]. Message posted to news://comp.edu.composition

28. SOFTWARE OR COMPUTER PROGRAM

PsychMate [Computer software]. (2003). Pittsburgh, PA: Psychology Software Tools.

Other Sources (Including Online Versions)

29. GOVERNMENT PUBLICATION

Office of the Federal Register. (2003). *The United States government manual 2003/2004*. Washington, DC: U.S. Government Printing Office.

For an online government document, add the date of access and the URL.

U.S. Public Health Service. (1999). *The surgeon general's call to
    action to prevent suicide.* Retrieved November 5, 2003, from
    http://www.mentalhealth.org/suicideprevention/calltoaction.asp

30. DISSERTATION ABSTRACT

If you use *Dissertation Abstracts International (DAI)*, include the *DAI*
volume, issue, and page number. If you use the UMI digital dissertation service, include the UMI number in parentheses but with no
period at the end of the entry.

Bandelj, N. (2003). Embedded economies: Foreign direct investment in
    Central and Eastern Europe. *Dissertation Abstracts International,
    64* (03), 1083. (UMI No. 3085036)

31. UNPUBLISHED DISSERTATION

Leverenz, C. A. (1994). *Collaboration and difference in the compo-
    sition classroom.* Unpublished doctoral dissertation, Ohio State
    University, Columbus.

32. TECHNICAL OR RESEARCH REPORT

Give the report number, if available, in parentheses after the title.

McCool, R., Fikes, R., & McGuinness, D. (2003). *Semantic web tools
    for enhanced authoring* (Report No. KSL-03-07). Stanford, CA:
    Knowledge Systems Laboratory.

33. CONFERENCE PROCEEDINGS

Mama, A. (2001). Challenging subjects: Gender and power in African
    contexts. In Proceedings of *Nordic African Institute Conference:
    Rethinking power in Africa.* Uppsala, Sweden, 9 – 18.

SOURCE MAP: Citing articles from databases using APA style

Libraries pay for services—such as InfoTrac, EBSCOhost, ProQuest, and LexisNexis—that provide access to large databases of electronic articles.

(1) *Author.* If available, include the author's name as you would for a print source. List all authors' last names first, and use only initials for first and middle names. Separate the names of multiple authors with commas, and use an ampersand (&) before the last author's name.

(2) *Publication date.* Enclose the date in parentheses. For journals, use only the year. For magazines and newspapers, use the year, a comma, the month (spelled out), and the day of the month if given.

(3) *Article title.* Do not italicize or enclose article titles in quotation marks. Capitalize only the first word of the article title and the subtitle and any proper nouns or proper adjectives.

(4) *Periodical title.* Italicize the periodical title (and subtitle, if any), and capitalize all major words.

(5) *Publication information.* Follow the periodical title with a comma, and then give the volume number (italicized) and, without a space in between, the issue number (if given) in parentheses.

(6) *Page numbers.* Give inclusive page numbers of the article. For newspapers, include abbreviation *p.* ("page") or *pp.* ("pages") before the page numbers.

(7) *Retrieval information.* Type the word *Retrieved* (or *Abstract retrieved,* for abstracts), followed by the date you retrieved the article and the name of the database.

(8) *Document number.* Provide a document number (sometimes called an article or accession number), if available, and end the citation with a period.

For a journal article retrieved from a database, use the following format:

Last name, First initial. (Year). Title of article. *Title of Journal, Volume number*(Issue number), Page number(s). Retrieved Month day, year, from Database name (Document number, if available).

A citation for the article on p. 215 would look like this:

VOLUME NUMBER, ITALICIZED, AND ISSUE NUMBER, IF GIVEN

AUTHORS' LAST NAMES, INITIALS   YEAR OF PUBLICATION   ARTICLE TITLE AND SUBTITLE, FIRST WORD OF EACH CAPITALIZED

Chory-Assad, R. M., & Tamborini, R. (2004). Television sitcom exposure and aggressive

PERIODICAL TITLE, ITALICIZED

communication: A priming perspective. *North American Journal of Psychology, 6*(3),

415–422. Retrieved August 8, 2005, from Academic Search Premier (15630823).

PAGE NUMBERS   RETRIEVAL DATE   DATABASE NAME   DOCUMENT NUMBER

DOUBLE-SPACE; INDENT ONE-HALF INCH OR FIVE SPACES

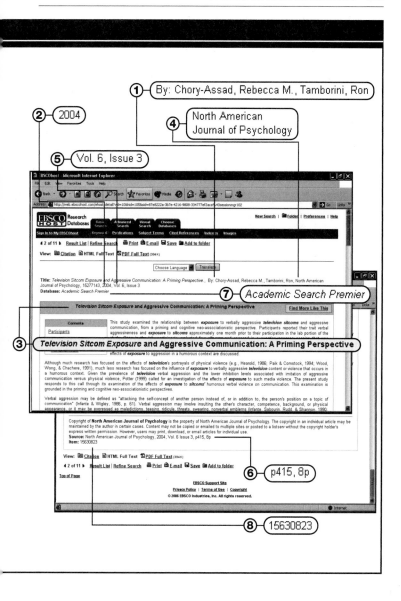

SOURCE MAP: Citing works from Web sites using APA style

(1) *Author.* If available, include the author's name as you would for a print source. List all authors' last names first, and use only initials for first and middle names. Separate the names of multiple authors with commas, and use an ampersand (&) before the last author's name. In some cases, the site's host or sponsoring organization may be the author. If no author is identified, begin the citation with the title of the document or Web site.

(2) *Publication date.* Include the date of Internet publication or latest update, if available. Use *n.d.* ("no date") when the publication date is unavailable.

(3) *Title.* Do not italicize or enclose document titles in quotation marks. Capitalize only the first word of the title and subtitle and any proper nouns or proper adjectives.

(4) *Retrieval information.* Type the word *Retrieved* followed by the date of access, a comma, and the word *from.* End with the URL and no period.

For a document found on a Web site with one author, use the following format:

Last name, First initial. (Internet publication date). Title of document. Retrieved Month
    day, year, from URL

A citation for the Web document on p. 217 would look like this:

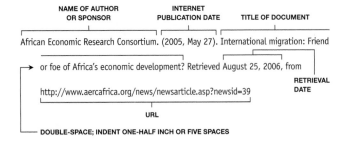

NAME OF AUTHOR   INTERNET
OR SPONSOR   PUBLICATION DATE   TITLE OF DOCUMENT

African Economic Research Consortium. (2005, May 27). International migration: Friend

or foe of Africa's economic development? Retrieved August 25, 2006, from

                                                      RETRIEVAL
    http://www.aercafrica.org/news/newsarticle.asp?newsid=39   DATE

                              URL

DOUBLE-SPACE; INDENT ONE-HALF INCH OR FIVE SPACES

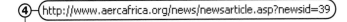

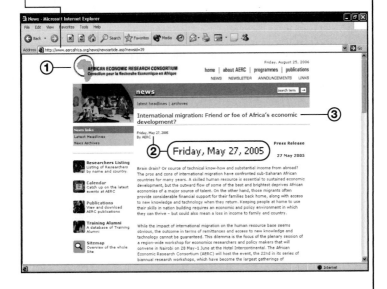

34. PAPER PRESENTED AT A MEETING OR SYMPOSIUM, UNPUBLISHED

Cite the month of the meeting if it is available.

Jones, J. G. (1999, February). *Mental health intervention in mass casualty disasters.* Paper presented at the Rocky Mountain Region Disaster Mental Health Conference, Laramie, WY.

35. POSTER SESSION

Barnes, Young, L. L. (2003, August). *Cognition, aging, and dementia.* Poster session presented at the 2003 Division 40 APA Convention, Toronto, Ontario, Canada.

36. FILM, VIDEO, OR DVD

Moore, M. (Director). (2003). *Bowling for Columbine* [Motion picture]. United States: MGM.

37. TELEVISION PROGRAM, SINGLE EPISODE

Imperioli, M. (Writer), & Buscemi, S. (Director). (2002). Everybody hurts [Television series episode]. In D. Chase (Executive Producer), *The Sopranos.* New York: HBO.

38. RECORDING

The Avalanches. (2001). Frontier psychiatrist. On *Since I left you* [CD]. Los Angeles: Elektra/Asylum Records.

A Student Research-Based Essay, APA Style

Student Writer

Merlla McLaughlin

On the following pages is a paper by Merlla McLaughlin that conforms to the APA guidelines described in this chapter. Note that this essay has been reproduced in a narrow format to accommodate the book's pocket size.

Leadership Roles   1

Leadership Roles in a Small-Group Project
Merlla McLaughlin
Professor Bushnell
Communications 102
February 22, 2004

Abstract

Using the interpersonal communications research of J. K. Brilhart and G. J. Galanes as well as that of W. Wilmot and J. Hocker, along with T. Hartman's Personality Assessment, I observed and analyzed the leadership roles and group dynamics of my project collaborators in a communications course. Based on results of the Hartman Personality Assessment, I predicted that a single leader would emerge. However, complementary individual strengths and gender differences encouraged a distributed leadership style, in which the group experienced little confrontation. Conflict, because it was handled positively, was crucial to the group's progress.

Leadership Roles in a Small-Group Project

Although classroom lectures provide students with volumes of information, many experiences can be understood only by living them. So it is with the workings of a small, task-focused group. What observations can I make after working with a group of peers on a class project? And what have I learned as a result?

Leadership Expectations and Emergence

The six members of this group were selected by the instructor; half were male and half were female. By performing the Hartman Personality Assessment (Hartman, 1998) in class, we learned that Hartman has associated key personality traits with the colors red, blue, white, and yellow (see Table 1). The assessment identified most of us as "Blues," concerned with intimacy and caring. Because of the bold qualities associated with "Reds," I expected that Nate, our only "Red" member, might become our leader. (Kaari, the only "White," seemed poised to become the peacekeeper.) However, after Nate missed the first two meetings, it seemed that Pat, who contributed often during our first three meetings, might emerge as leader. Pat has strong communications skills, a commanding presence, and displays sensitivity

Table 1

Hartman's Key Personality Traits

Trait category	Color			
	Red	Blue	White	Yellow
Motive	Power	Intimacy	Peace	Fun
Strengths	Loyal to tasks	Loyal to people	Tolerant	Positive
Limitations	Arrogant	Self-righteous	Timid	Uncommitted

Note. Table is adapted from information found at The Hartman Personality Profile, by N. Hayden. Retrieved February 24, 2004, from http://students.cs.byu.edu/~nhayden/Code/index.php

to others. I was surprised, then, when our group developed a *distributed* style of leadership (Brilhart & Galanes, 1998). The longer we worked together, however, the more I was convinced that this approach to leadership was best for our group.

As Brilhart and Galanes have noted, "distributed leadership explicitly acknowledges that the leadership of a group is spread among members, with each member expected to move the group toward its goal" (p. 175). These researchers divide positive communicative actions into two types: *task functions* that affect a group's productivity and *maintenance functions* that influence the interactions of group members. One of our group's most immediate task-function needs was decision-making, and as we made our first major decision — what topic to pursue — our group's distributed-leadership style began to emerge.

Decision-Making Methods

Our choice of topic — the parking services at Oregon State University (OSU) — was the result not of a majority vote but of negotiated consensus. During this decision-making meeting, several of us argued that a presentation on parking services at OSU would interest most students, and after considerable discussion, the other group members agreed. Once we had a topic, other decisions came naturally.

Roles Played

Thanks in part to the distributed leadership that our group developed, the strengths of individual group members became increasingly apparent. Although early in our project Pat was the key initiator and Nate was largely an information seeker, all group members eventually took on these functions in addition to serving as recorders, gathering information, and working on our questionnaire. Every member coordinated the group's work at some point; several made sure that everyone could speak and be heard, and one member was especially good at catching important details the rest of us were apt to miss. Joe, McKenzie, Kaari, and I frequently clarified or elaborated on information, whereas Pat, Kaari, and Nate were good at contributing ideas during brainstorming sessions. Nate, Joe, and McKenzie brought tension-relieving humor to the group.

Just as each member brought individual strengths to the group, gender differences also made us effective. For example, the women took a holistic approach to the project, looking at the big picture and making intuitive leaps in ways that the men generally did not. The men preferred a more systematic process. Brilhart and Galanes have suggested that men working in groups dominated by women may display "subtle forms of resistance to a dominant presence of women" (p. 98). Although the men in our group did not attend all the meetings and the women did, I did not find that the men's nonattendance implied male resistance any more than the women's attendance implied female dominance. Rather, our differing qualities complemented each other and enabled us to work together effectively.

Social Environment

As previously noted, most of our group members were Blues on the Hartman scale, valuing altruism, intimacy, appreciation, and having a moral conscience (Hayden). At least three of the four Blues had White as their secondary color, signifying the importance of peace, kindness, independence, and sacrifice (Hayden). The presence of these traits may explain why our group experienced little confrontation and conflict. Nate (a Red) was most likely to speak bluntly. The one time that Nate seemed put off, it was not his words but his body language that expressed his discomfort. This was an awkward moment, but a rare one given our group's generally positive handling of conflict.

Conclusion

Perhaps most important is the lesson I learned about conflict. Prior to participating in this group, I always avoided conflict because, as Wilmot and Hocker (1998) have suggested, most people think "harmony is normal and conflict is abnormal" (p. 9). Now I recognize that some kinds of conflict are essential for increasing

Leadership Roles   8

understanding between group members and creating an effective collaborative result. It was essential, for instance, that our group explore different members' ideas about possible topics for our project, and this process inevitably required some conflict. The end result, however, was a positive one.

Constructive conflict requires an open and engaging attitude among group members, encourages personal growth, and ends when the issue at hand is resolved. Most important for our group, such conflict encouraged cooperation (pp. 47 – 48) and increased the group's cohesiveness. All the members of our group felt, for instance, that their ideas about possible topics were seriously considered. Once we decided on a topic, everyone fully committed to it. Thus our group effectiveness was enhanced by constructive conflict.

As a result of this project, I have a better sense of when conflict is — and isn't — productive. My group used conflict productively when we hashed out our ideas, and we avoided the kind of conflict that creates morale problems and wastes time. Although all groups operate somewhat differently, I now feel more prepared to understand and participate in future small-group projects.

Leadership Roles   9

References

Brilhart, J. K., & Galanes, G. J. (1998). *Effective group discussion* (9th ed.). Boston: McGraw-Hill.

Hartman, T. (1998). *The color code: A new way to see yourself, your relationships, and your life*. New York: Scribner.

Hayden, N. (n.d.). *The Hartman Personality Profile*. Retrieved February 15, 2004, from http://students .cs.byu.edu/~nhayden/Code/index.php

Wilmot, W., & Hocker, J. (1998). *Interpersonal conflict* (5th ed.) Boston: McGraw-Hill.

7

Research in the Natural and Physical Sciences and in Mathematics

Resources in the Natural and Physical Sciences and in Mathematics

GENERAL REFERENCE SOURCES FOR THE NATURAL AND PHYSICAL SCIENCES AND FOR MATHEMATICS

CRC Handbook of Chemistry and Physics. 1913–. Supplies frequently used formulas, constants, properties of elements and compounds, atomic weights, and numerous illustrative charts and tables for reference. (online)

Encyclopedia of Physical Science and Technology. 18 vols. 2001. Supplies extensive articles on topics in the physical sciences and technology, including bibliographies, glossaries, and illustrations. (online)

McGraw-Hill Dictionary of Scientific and Technical Terms. 2003. Supplies pronunciations and definitions for thousands of terms used in the pure and applied sciences. (CD-ROM)

McGraw-Hill Encyclopedia of Science and Technology. 20 vols. 2002. Supplies articles with bibliographies and illustrations for extensive coverage of topics in all scientific fields, with updated coverage of the earth sciences, environmental studies, engineering, medicine, chemistry, and other rapidly developing fields; many smaller specialized McGraw-Hill scientific encyclopedias derive from this major work. (online)

Van Nostrand's Scientific Encyclopedia. 2 vols. 2002. Supplies articles explaining and defining a wide variety of terms and topics in the sciences, medicine, and mathematics. (online)

INDEXES AND DATABASES FOR THE NATURAL AND PHYSICAL SCIENCES AND FOR MATHEMATICS

Abstracts and Indexes in Science and Technology: A Descriptive Guide. 1985. Supplies detailed information on specialized abstracts and indexes available for the various scientific disciplines.

General Science Index. 1978–. Indexes and abstracts over one hundred periodicals covering the sciences, mathematics, medicine, environmental studies, and related topics. (online)

Information Sources in Science and Technology. 1998. Annotated guide to general and specialized resources for twenty-one scientific, medical, and technological disciplines. (online)

Science Citation Index. 1955–. Indexes and abstracts citations in articles from over three thousand scientific periodicals; entries allow tracing influence through the frequency of later citations by other researchers. (online)

WEB RESOURCES FOR THE NATURAL AND PHYSICAL SCIENCES AND FOR MATHEMATICS

EurekAlert! Your Global Gateway to Science, Medicine, and Technology News
www.eurekalert.org
Under the sponsorship of the American Association for the Advancement of Science, posts news of scientific, medical, and technological research advances; also includes glossaries, dictionaries, and other reference materials for major scientific fields.

Infomine: Scholarly Internet Resource Collections
infomine.ucr.edu
Supplies indexed and annotated links to databases and other resources of academic interest in biology, medicine, mathematics, and the physical sciences.

New Scientist
www.newscientist.com
> Supplies engaging annotated links to selected sites in many scientific fields, including specialized topics.

NIST (National Institute of Standards and Technology) Virtual Library
nvl.nist.gov
> Includes extensive links to sites, databases, and journals in many fields, including biotechnology, chemistry, mathematics, computer science, engineering, and physics.

Science Online
www.sciencemag.org
> Includes the online version of *Science,* published weekly by the American Association for the Advancement of Science, and provides free access to current news about scientific advances and career information.

The Webliography: Internet Subject Guides
www.lib.lsu.edu/weblio.html
> Provides extensive annotated guides to Web resources in the sciences, including biology, chemistry, earth sciences, history of science, medicine, physics, and specialized fields.

(See also the resources listed for the applied sciences in Chapter 8.)

Astronomy

GENERAL REFERENCE SOURCES FOR ASTRONOMY

Encyclopedia of Astronomy and Astrophysics. 2001. Supplies extensive articles, including glossaries and bibliographies, on major topics in these fields. (online at http://www.ency-astro.com/)

INDEXES AND DATABASES FOR ASTRONOMY

ARIBIB-ARI Bibliographic Database for Astronomical Reference. 1969–2000. Ceased in print. Formerly *Astronomisches Jahresbericht,* 1900–1968. Indexes and abstracts articles from periodicals, books, papers, and other materials, extensively covering astronomy, space research, astrophysics, planets, stars, and related topics. (online)

WEB RESOURCES FOR ASTRONOMY

AstronomyCafe
www.astronomycafe.com
>Provides varied resources about astronomy, including questions and answers for astronomers and space scientists, career information, and an extensive list of links to related sites.

The Astronomy Net
www.astronomy.net
>Includes links to recent news stories and articles, as well as discussion groups and clubs.

AstroWeb: Astronomy/Astrophysics on the Internet
www.cv.nrao.edu/fits/www/astronomy.html
>Provides one version of the AstroWeb, a collaborative database of over two thousand items available at several sites, here sorted by such categories as images, observations, data, publications, organizations, people, and research specialties.

NASA Web
www.nasa.gov
>Covers the aerospace program, space and earth sciences, technology applications, and topics such as shuttles and space stations; also provides links to other NASA resources and images.

The Star*s Family of Astronomy and Related Resources—The StarPages
vizier.u-strasbg.fr/starsfamily.html
>Includes thousands of entries, including abbreviations, symbols, and personal Web pages, as well as links to many organizations and resources.

WebStars—Astrophysics in Cyberspace
heasarc.gsfc.nasa.gov/docs/www_info/webstars.html
>Supplies engaging annotations and images for links to astronomy, the solar system, and space exploration.

The WWW Virtual Library—Astronomy and Astrophysics & AstroWeb
www.astroweb.com.ar
>Supplies an impressive range of links to resources, observatories, organizations, publications, data, and images in astronomy and related fields.

Chemistry

GENERAL REFERENCE SOURCES FOR CHEMISTRY

Kirk-Othmer Encyclopedia of Chemical Technology. 27 vols. 2004–. Supplies hundreds of articles on the properties and uses of chemical substances as well as on other topics related to chemical processes, methods, and technology. (online)

Van Nostrand Encyclopedia of Chemistry. 2005. Available in print and online. Supplies articles on chemistry-related topics as diverse as food chemistry, plant chemistry, pollution, and energy sources.

INDEXES AND DATABASES FOR CHEMISTRY

Chemical Abstracts. 1907–. Indexes and abstracts articles from over fourteen thousand periodicals, as well as books, reports, and other materials covering all major chemical fields. (online)

Chemical Reviews. 1924–. 8/yr. Covers all areas of chemistry; includes comprehensive bibliographies. (online)

How to Find Chemical Information: A Guide for Practicing Chemists, Educators, and Students. 1998. Explains the contents of and ways to use major print and electronic resources in chemistry. (online)

WEB RESOURCES FOR CHEMISTRY

ACSWEB
acswebcontent.acs.org/home.html
> Provides searches of American Chemical Society resources as well as information on news, events, and publications.

CHEMINFO
www.indiana.edu/~cheminfo/cisindex.html
> Chemical Information Sources from Indiana University is a guide to Internet and Web resources in chemistry; offers both alphabetical and keyword searches in a useful format.

Molecular Visualization Tools and Sites
www.indiana.edu/~cheminfo/ca_mvts.html
> Links to all the major Chime and RasMol sites as well as to various other free and commercial visualization sites.

The WWW Virtual Library—Chemistry
www.liv.ac.uk/Chemistry/Links/links.html
> Links to universities and organizations as well as to chemistry resources and other virtual libraries.

Earth Sciences

GENERAL REFERENCE SOURCES FOR EARTH SCIENCES

A Dictionary of Earth Sciences. 2003. Includes over six thousand entries covering fields such as climatology, exonomic geology, geochemistry, oceanography, petrology, and volanology. (online)

Encyclopedia of Earth Sciences. c. 24 vols. 1966–. Supplies articles in volumes focused on specific topics, including oceanography, mineralogy, paleontology, geology, climatology, and other specialized areas.

Encyclopedia of Earth System Science. 4 vols. 1992. Provides thorough coverage of topics in this specialized field.

Encyclopedia of Minerals. 2nd ed. 1990–. Supplies descriptions and some color photographs of more than twenty-five hundred minerals.

The Facts on File Dictionary of Earth Science. 2006. Lists general definitions of over thirty-seven hundred terms; includes cross-references.

McGraw-Hill Dictionary of Earth Science. 2003. Defines thousands of terms used in the various engineering fields, geology, mineralogy, crystallography, and paleontology. (online)

McGraw-Hill Dictionary of Geology and Mineralogy. 2003. Contains over seven thousand terms and expressions, each arranged under the field of geology and mineralogy in which it is used, including physical and historical geology, plate tectonics, and petrology. (online)

INDEXES AND DATABASES FOR EARTH SCIENCES

Bibliography and Index of Geology. 1969–. Ceased in print 2005. Formerly *Bibliography of North American Geology*, 1931–1972, and *Bibliography and Index of Geology Exclusive of North America*, 1933–1968. Indexes articles on many geological topics, supplying extensive coverage of the field. (online)

WEB RESOURCES FOR EARTH SCIENCES

CIESIN: Information for a Changing World
www.ciesin.org
> Consolidates scientific data, interactive services, and access to resources on the global environment, under the auspices of the Consortium for International Earth Science Information Network.

GeologyLink
www.geologylink.com
> Provides, under the sponsorship of the publisher Houghton Mifflin, news, current events, visits to geologic sites, a forum on geology, and links to course materials, references, glossaries, and other Web sites.

Hawaii Center for Volcanology
www.soest.hawaii.edu/GG/hcv.html
> Provides links to numerous volcano sites, including the Hawaiian Volcano Observatory, NASA's Virtually Hawaii project, and a virtual voyage to Puna Ridge, a volcanic ridge three miles under the sea.

Internet Resources in the Earth Sciences
www.lib.berkeley.edu/EART/EarthLinks.html
> An annotated list of sites in the earth sciences and more specialized fields such as seismology, weather, and oceanography.

NASA's Global Change Master Directory (GCMD)
gcmd.gsfc.nasa.gov
> Allows keyword searches and includes many links to other earth science sources.

National Geophysical Data Center
www.ngdc.noaa.gov
> Supplies information—including satellite data—for environmental studies and specialized fields such as marine geology, glaciology, and paleoclimatology.

USGS (United States Geological Survey): Science for a Changing World
www.usgs.gov
> Provides highlights, fact sheets, information on federal programs and initiatives, and access to extensive resources and databases on geology, biology, water resources, mapping, and related topics.

The WWW Virtual Library—Earth Sciences
www.vlib.org/EarthScience.html
Categorizes its numerous links by subject; includes many subdisciplines such as oceanography and meteorology.

Life Sciences

GENERAL REFERENCE SOURCES FOR LIFE SCIENCES

Encyclopedia of Bioethics. 3rd ed. 5 vols. 2004. Includes articles on life science ethics, policies, legal issues, religious perspectives, and related issues. (online)

Encyclopedia of Human Biology. 2nd ed. 9 vols. 1997. Provides hundreds of extensive articles on biological topics as diverse as anthropology, biochemistry, ecology, genetics, and physiology.

The Encyclopedia of Mammals. 2006. Entries cover every living species of mammal; emphasize animal behavior, conservation, and ecology; and are accompanied by over eight hundred full-color illustrations.

Encyclopedia of Microbiology. 4 vols. 2000. Supplies thorough coverage of topics in this specialized field. (online)

Grzimek's Animal Life Encyclopedia. 17 vols. 2003–2004. Provides articles and illustrations on the various kinds of animal life. (online)

Grzimek's Encyclopedia of Mammals. 5 vols. 1989. Supplies photographs and articles with bibliographies on mammal groups, including detailed coverage of many species.

Oxford Dictionary of Natural History. 1985. Provides thousands of definitions and explanations about the various types of plants and animals, plus genetics, biochemistry, and earth sciences. (online)

Walker's Mammals of the World. 2 vols. 1999. Supplies entries, many illustrated, on mammal types, and includes a bibliography of sources cited.

INDEXES AND DATABASES FOR LIFE SCIENCES

Biological Abstracts. 1926–. Indexes and abstracts articles from roughly ninety-five hundred periodicals, comprehensively covering biology and biomedicine. (online)

Biological and Agricultural Index. 1964–. Formerly *Agricultural Index*, 1916–1964. Indexes over 250 periodicals covering a wide range of agricultural and biological topics such as animal husbandry, zoology, genetics, botany, food production, and environmental studies. (online)

Cumulative Index to Nursing and Allied Health Literature. 1961–. Indexes and abstracts hundreds of periodicals on nursing and related health areas. (online)

Index Medicus. 1899–1926; 1960–2002. Formerly *Quarterly Cumulative Index Medicus*, 1927–1959. Indexes thousands of major medical and health care periodicals, excluding popular magazines. (online as PubMed at http://www.ncbi.nlm.nih.gov/entrez/query.fcgi?db=PubMed)

WEB RESOURCES FOR LIFE SCIENCES

Biosciences Index
mcb.harvard.edu/BioLinks.html
> Allows searching by keyword and provides an alphabetical list of links for specialties within the biosciences.

Biosciences Web Resources
www.herts.ac.uk/lis/subjects/natsci/bio/bioweb
> Includes links to sites in the biosciences, from biochemistry to physiology, as well as links to reference works, journals, magazines, and newsletters in the field.

Centers for Disease Control and Prevention
www.cdc.gov
> The home page of the famous virus hunters, with links to what they do, search facilities, other sites, and a wide range of useful government data.

Human Genome Project
www.genome.gov
> The home page for this important research project; situated at the National Institutes of Health.

Links to the Genetic World
www.ornl.gov/hgmis/links.html
> Provides basic and specialized information on genetics and the Human Genome Project, as well as keyword searches and links to numerous genetics-related sites.

National Institutes of Health
www.nih.gov
> The central government organization dealing with health issues; site includes news, health information, grant descriptions, and links to scientific resources and to NIH suborganizations.

National Science Foundation: Biology
www.nsf.gov/index.jsp
> The site of the primary government agency funding scientific research. Allows a search of its Biology Directorate's sources and includes links to online documents, grants, and specific fields within biology.

NetVet
netvet.wustl.edu
> From the Washington University Division of Comparative Medicine, NetVet includes links to special fields in veterinary medicine, numerous sites for particular animals, and an electronic zoo.

Nursing
www.atnursing.com/nursing
> Allows keyword searches and includes annotated sites for nursing and other medical-related fields.

Pasteur Institute
www.pasteur.fr/english.html
> Allows keyword searches of the Pasteur Institute's server and many other English language–based bioscience servers.

Scott's Botanical Links
www.ou.edu/cas/botany-micro/bot-linx
> Includes annotated lists of databases and detailed descriptions of links to other botanical sites.

The WWW Virtual Library—Biosciences
vlib.org/Biosciences.html
> Categorizes information by provider and subject. A good place to begin research, this site includes many links to journals, subdisciplines, and related sites.

(See also the resources listed for agriculture in Chapter 8 on the applied sciences.)

Mathematics

GENERAL REFERENCE SOURCES FOR MATHEMATICS

CRC Handbook of Mathematical Sciences. 1987. Supplies frequently used mathematical functions, equations, factors, formulas, measurements, statistics, and abbreviations.

Encyclopedic Dictionary of Mathematics. 4 vols. 1987. Includes articles defining many mathematical terms and topics.

INDEXES AND DATABASES FOR MATHEMATICS

Mathematical Reviews. 1940–. Indexes and abstracts extensive resources in all areas of mathematics, including theory, history, probability, games, circuits, and related topics. (online as *Math on the Web*)

WEB RESOURCES FOR MATHEMATICS

American Mathematical Society, Mathematics on the Web
www.ams.org/mathweb
> Offers literature guides and links both on- and offline, references, topical guides, and links to individuals.

Eric's Treasure Trove of Mathematics
mathworld.wolfram.com
> An alphabetical search list of important terms and concepts.

Materials Organized by Mathematical Topics
www.ams.org/mathweb/mi-mathbytopic.html
> Links to specific issues in current mathematical work.

Math Archives Bibliographies
archives.math.utk.edu/cgi-bin/bibliography.html
> Lists bibliographies and subject links; supplements the Math Archives home page.

Math Archives: Topics in Mathematics
archives.math.utk.edu/topics
> Devoted to math issues of special interest to undergraduate students. Includes societies, projects, research, competitions, and career issues.

Math Forum Internet Mathematics Library
mathforum.org/library
> Provides extensive links to all areas of mathematics, including math education from elementary through college levels.

MathSearch
www.maths.usyd.edu.au/MathSearch.html
> Searches over ninety thousand documents on English-language math and statistics servers, keying by phrase.

The Most Common Errors in Undergraduate Mathematics
www.math.vanderbilt.edu/~schectex/commerrs
> From Eric Schecter at Vanderbilt University.

(See also the resources listed for engineering in Chapter 8 on the applied sciences.)

Physics

GENERAL REFERENCE SOURCES FOR PHYSICS

American Institute of Physics Handbook. 1972. Supplies formulas and other reference materials, specifically selected for the physicist.

Encyclopedia of Physics. 2004. Includes extensive articles written for a general audience on major topics in the field. (online)

Handbook of Physics. 2006. Contains fundamental concepts, formulas, rules, theorems, and tables of standard values and material properties; topics discussed include classical mathematics, elementary particles, electric circuits, and error analysis.

McGraw-Hill Dictionary of Physics. 2003. Defines thousands of key terms from eighteen areas of physics and other closely connected fields. (online)

INDEXES AND DATABASES FOR PHYSICS

Information Sources in Physics. 3rd ed. 1994. Supplies entries on print and electronic resources in physics.

Physics Abstracts. 1898–. Indexes and abstracts periodicals and other resources in major areas of physics and in related scientific fields. (online)

WEB RESOURCES FOR PHYSICS

AIP Physics Information
www.aip.org
> Links to societies, publications, career services, and databases from the American Institute of Physics.

American Physical Society
www.aps.org
> Allows quick access to professional activities and databases.

Contemporary Physics Education Project
www.cpepweb.org
> Provides links to several interactive explanations of fields in physics and lists of other sites.

HEPIC Global Search
www.hep.net/search/hepic.html
> Covers all the major electronic databases in physics, using a keyword search.

NASA
www.nasa.gov
> The home page contains useful links to current NASA projects.

The Net Advance of Physics
www.mit.edu/redingtn/www/netadv
> Includes the *Physicist's Encyclopedia,* a collection of review articles in physics arranged by subject.

Physics News
www.het.brown.edu/news/index.html
> Lists the latest work being done in physics, including NASA's *Hot Topics* and the newsletter *The Scientist,* science news from wire services, and links to other journals and magazines.

PhysicsWeb
physicsweb.org
> Allows access to physics societies, databases, projects, news, and events.

PhysLink.com
www.physlink.com
> Contains articles on current news items, links to journals and physics departments, and a question-and-answer feature.

U.S. Department of Energy
www.energy.gov
> Contains data on current research and developments in physics; subsidized by the Department of Energy.

The WWW Virtual Library—Physics
www.vlib.org/Physics.html
> Categorizes its links by subject.

CSE Style

Writers in the physical sciences, the life sciences, and mathematics use the documentation and format style of the Council of Science Editors (CSE). Guidelines for citing print and electronic sources can be found in *Scientific Style and Format: The CSE Manual for Authors, Editors, and Publishers*, Seventh Edition (2006).

CSE Formats for In-Text Citations

In CSE style, citations within an essay follow one of three formats.

- The *citation-sequence format* calls for a superscript number or a number in parentheses after any mention of a source. The sources are numbered in the order they appear. Each number refers to the same source every time it is used. The first source mentioned in the paper is numbered *1*, the second source is numbered *2*, and so on.

- The *citation-name format* also calls for a superscript number or a number in parentheses after any mention of a source. The numbers are added after the list of references is completed and alphabetized, so that the source numbered *1* is alphabetically first in the list of references, *2* is alphabetically second, and so on.

- The *name-year format* calls for the last name of the author and the year of publication in parentheses after any mention of a source. If the last name appears in a signal phrase, the name-year format allows for giving only the year of publication in parentheses.

Before deciding which system to use, check a current journal in the field or ask an instructor about the preferred style in a particular course or discipline.

**1. IN-TEXT CITATION USING CITATION-SEQUENCE
OR CITATION-NAME FORMAT**

VonBergen[12] provides the most complete discussion of this phenomenon.

For the citation-sequence and citation-name formats, you would use the same superscript[12] for each subsequent citation of this work by VonBergen.

2. IN-TEXT CITATION USING NAME-YEAR FORMAT

VonBergen (2003) provides the most complete discussion of this phenomenon.

Hussar's two earlier studies of juvenile obesity (1995, 1999) examined only children with diabetes.

The classic examples of such investigations (Morrow 1968; Bridger et al. 1971; Franklin and Wayson 1972) still shape the assumptions of current studies.

CSE Formats for a List of References

The citations in the text of an essay correspond to items on a list titled *References*, which starts on a new page at the end of the essay. Continue to number the pages consecutively, center the title *References* one inch from the top of the page, and double-space before beginning the first entry.

The order of the entries depends on which CSE format you follow:

- *Citation-sequence format*: number and list the references in the order the references are first cited in the text.
- *Citation-name format*: list and number the references in alphabetical order.
- *Name-year format*: list the references, unnumbered, in alphabetical order.

In the following examples, you will see that the citation-sequence and citation-name formats call for listing the date after the publisher's name in references for books and after the periodical name in references for articles. The name-year format calls for listing the date immediately after the author's name in any kind of reference.

CSE style also specifies the treatment and placement of the following basic elements in the list of references:

- *Author*. List all authors last name first, and use only initials for first and middle names. Do not place a comma after the author's last name, and do not place periods after or spaces between the initials. Use a period after the last initial of the last author listed.
- *Title*. Do not italicize or underline titles and subtitles of books and titles of periodicals. Do not enclose titles of articles in quotation marks. For books and articles, capitalize only the first word of the title and any proper nouns or proper adjectives. Abbreviate and capitalize all major words in a periodical title.

As you refer to these examples, pay attention to how publication information (publishers for books, details about periodicals for articles) and other specific elements are styled and punctuated.

DIRECTORY TO CSE STYLE FOR REFERENCES

BOOKS

PERIODICALS

ELECTRONIC SOURCES

Books

For the basic format for citing a book, see pp. 246–47.

1. ONE AUTHOR

CITATION-SEQUENCE AND CITATION-NAME

1. Buchanan M. Nexus: small worlds and the groundbreaking theory of networks. New York: Norton; 2003.

NAME-YEAR

Buchanan M. 2003. Nexus: small worlds and the groundbreaking theory of networks. New York: Norton.

SOURCE MAP: Citing books using CSE style

Note that, depending on whether you are using the citation-sequence or citation-name format or the name-year format, the date placement will vary.

(1) *Author.* List authors' last names first, and use initials for first and middle names. Do not place periods after or spaces between initials. Use a period after the last initial of the last author.

(2),(6) *Publication year.* In name-year format, put the year of publication immediately after the author name(s). In citation-sequence or citation-name format, put the year of publication after the publisher's name.

(3) *Title.* Do not italicize, underline, or put quotation marks around titles and subtitles of books. Capitalize only the first word of the title and any proper nouns or proper adjectives.

(4) *City of publication.* List the city of publication (and the country or state abbreviation for unfamiliar cities) followed by a colon.

(5) *Publisher.* Give the publisher's name. In citation-sequence or citation-name format, follow with a semicolon. In name-year format, follow with a period.

For a book by one author with no middle initial, use one of the following formats:

Citation-sequence or citation-name format

1. Last name and first initial(s). Title of book: subtitle. City: Publisher; Year.

Name-year format

Last name and first initial(s). Year. Title of book: subtitle. City: Publisher.

A citation for the book on p. 247 would look like this:

Citation-sequence or citation-name format

| NOTE
NUMBER | AUTHOR'S NAME
AND INITIALS | TITLE AND SUBTITLE
(IF ANY) |

1. Willett WC. Eat, drink, and be healthy: the Harvard Medical School guide to healthy eating. New York: Free Press; 2001.   DOUBLE-SPACE; NO INDENT

CITY OF PUBLICATION   PUBLISHER   PUBLICATION YEAR

Name-year format

Willett WC. 2001. Eat, drink, and be healthy: the Harvard Medical School guide to healthy eating. New York: Free Press.

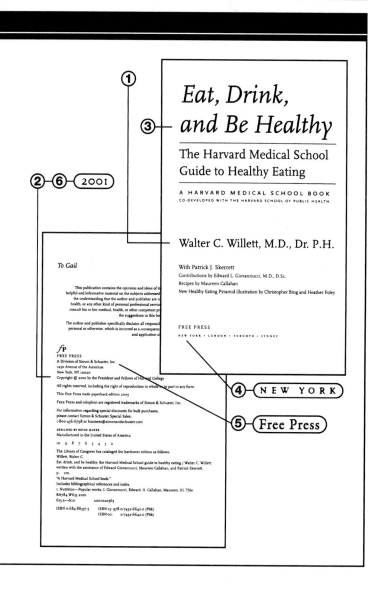

① *Eat, Drink, and Be Healthy*

③ *and Be Healthy*

The Harvard Medical School
Guide to Healthy Eating

A HARVARD MEDICAL SCHOOL BOOK
CO-DEVELOPED WITH THE HARVARD SCHOOL OF PUBLIC HEALTH

② ⑥ 2001

Walter C. Willett, M.D., Dr. P.H.

With Patrick J. Skerrett
Contributions by Edward L. Giovannucci, M.D., D.Sc.
Recipes by Maureen Callahan
New Healthy Eating Pyramid illustration by Christopher Bing and Heather Foley

To Gail

This publication contains the opinions and ideas of its
helpful and informative material on the subjects addressed
the understanding that the author and publisher are n
health, or any other kind of personal professional servic
consult his or her medical, health, or other competent pr
the suggestions in this bo

The author and publisher specifically disclaim all responsibi
personal or otherwise, which is incurred as a consequenc
and application o

FREE PRESS

NEW YORK · LONDON · TORONTO · SYDNEY

④ NEW YORK

⑤ Free Press

ƒP
FREE PRESS
A Division of Simon & Schuster, Inc.
1230 Avenue of the Americas
New York, NY 10020

Copyright © 2001 by the President and Fellows of Harvard College

All rights reserved, including the right of reproduction in whole or in part in any form.

This Free Press trade paperback edition 2005

FREE PRESS and colophon are registered trademarks of Simon & Schuster, Inc.

For information regarding special discounts for bulk purchases,
please contact Simon & Schuster Special Sales:
1-800-456-6798 or business@simonandschuster.com

DESIGNED BY KEVIN HANEK
Manufactured in the United States of America

10 9 8 7 6 5 4 3 2

The Library of Congress has cataloged the hardcover edition as follows:
Willett, Walter C.
Eat, drink, and be healthy: the Harvard Medical School guide to healthy eating / Walter C. Willett;
written with the assistance of Edward Giovannucci, Maureen Callahan, and Patrick Skerrett.
p. cm.
"A Harvard Medical School book."
Includes bibliographical references and index.
1. Nutrition—Popular works. I. Giovannucci, Edward. II. Callahan, Maureen. III. Title.
RA784.W6335 2001
613.2—dc21   2001020565

ISBN 0-684-86337-5   ISBN-13: 978-0-7432-6642-0 (Pbk)
                         ISBN-10:   0-7432-6642-0 (Pbk)

2. TWO OR MORE AUTHORS

CITATION-SEQUENCE AND CITATION-NAME

2. Wojciechowski BW, Rice NM. Experimental methods in kinetic studies. 2nd ed. St. Louis (MO): Elsevier Science; 2003.

NAME-YEAR

Wojciechowski BW, Rice NM. 2003. Experimental methods in kinetic studies. 2nd ed. St. Louis (MO): Elsevier Science.

3. ORGANIZATION AS AUTHOR

CITATION-SEQUENCE AND CITATION-NAME

3. World Health Organization. The world health report 2002: reducing risks, promoting healthy life. Geneva (Switzerland): The Organization; 2002.

Place the organization's abbreviation at the beginning of the name-year entry, and use the abbreviation in the corresponding in-text citation. Alphabetize the entry by the first word of the full name, not by the abbreviation.

NAME-YEAR

[WHO] World Health Organization. 2002. The world health report 2002: reducing risks, promoting healthy life. Geneva (Switzerland): The Organization.

4. BOOK PREPARED BY EDITOR(S)

CITATION-SEQUENCE AND CITATION-NAME

4. Torrence ME, Isaacson RE, editors. Microbial food safety in animal agriculture: current topics. Ames: Iowa State University Press; 2003.

NAME-YEAR

Torrence ME, Isaacson RE, editors. 2003. Microbial safety in animal agriculture: current topics. Ames: Iowa State University Press.

5. SECTION OF A BOOK WITH AN EDITOR

CITATION-SEQUENCE AND CITATION-NAME

5. Kawamura A. Plankton. In: Perrin MF, Wursig B, Thewissen JGM, editors. Encyclopedia of marine mammals. San Diego: Academic Press; 2002. p. 939–942.

NAME-YEAR

Kawamura A. 2002. Plankton. In: Perrin MF, Wursig B, Thewissen JGM, editors. Encyclopedia of marine mammals. San Diego: Academic Press. p. 939–942.

6. CHAPTER OF A BOOK

CITATION-SEQUENCE AND CITATION-NAME

6. Honigsbaum M. The fever trail: in search of the cure for malaria. New York: Picador; 2003. Chapter 2, The cure; p. 19–38.

NAME-YEAR

Honigsbaum M. 2003. The fever trail: in search of the cure for malaria. New York: Picador. Chapter 2, The cure; p. 19–38.

7. PAPER OR ABSTRACT IN CONFERENCE PROCEEDINGS

CITATION-SEQUENCE AND CITATION-NAME

7. Gutierrez AP. Integrating biological and environmental factors in crop system models [abstract]. In: Integrated Biological Systems Conference; 2003 Apr 14–16; San Antonio, TX. Beaumont (TX): Agroeconomics Research Group; 2003. p. 14–15.

NAME-YEAR

Gutierrez AP. 2003. Integrating biological and environmental factors in crop system models [abstract]. In: Integrated Biological Systems Conference; 2003 Apr 14–16; San Antonio, TX. Beaumont (TX): Agroeconomics Research Group. p. 14–15.

SOURCE MAP: Citing articles from periodicals using CSE style

Note that date placement will vary, depending on whether you are using the citation-sequence or citation-name format or the name-year format.

(1) *Author.* List all authors' last names first, and use only initials for first and middle names. Do not place periods after or spaces betwen the initials. Use a period after the last initial of the last author.

(2),(5) *Publication date.* In name-year format, put publication date after author name(s). In citation-sequence or citation-name format, put publication date after periodical title. For journals, use only the year; use the year and month (and day) for publications without volume numbers.

(3) *Title and subtitle of article.* Capitalize only the first word of the title and any proper nouns or proper adjectives.

(4) *Title of periodical.* Capitalize all major words and end with a period. Follow the guidelines in the CSE manual for abbreviating journal titles.

(6) *Publication information.* For articles from scholarly journals, give the volume number, the issue number if available (in parentheses), and then a colon.

(7) *Page numbers.* Give the inclusive page numbers, and end with a period.

For an article in a scholarly journal, use one of the following formats:

Citation-sequence or citation-name format

1. Last name first initial. Title of article. Journal abbreviation. Year;Volume(Issue):Pages.

Name-year format

Last name first initial. Year. Title of article. Journal abbreviation. Volume(Issue):Pages.

Citations for the article on p. 251 would look like this:

Citation-sequence or citation-name format

NOTE   AUTHOR'S LAST   ARTICLE TITLE AND SUBTITLE
NUMBER   NAME AND INITIAL   (IF ANY)

1. Narechania A. Hearing is believing: ivory-billed sightings leave field biologists

wanting to hear more. Am Scholar. 2005;74(3):84-97.   DOUBLE-SPACE; NO INDENT

JOURNAL TITLE   PUBLICATION   VOLUME AND   PAGE NUMBERS
ABBREVIATED   YEAR   ISSUE NUMBERS

Name-Year format

Narechania A. 2005. Hearing is believing: ivory-billed sightings leave field biologists wanting to hear more. Am Scholar. 74(3):84-97.

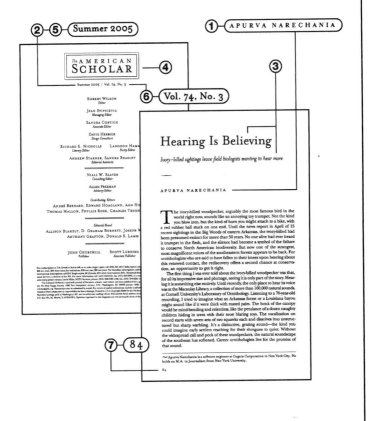

Periodicals

For the basic format for an article from a periodical, see pp. 250–51. For newspaper and magazine articles, include the section designation and column number, if any, in addition to the date and the inclusive page numbers. For rules on abbreviating journal titles, consult the CSE manual, or ask an instructor to suggest other examples.

8. ARTICLE IN A JOURNAL

CITATION-SEQUENCE AND CITATION-NAME

8. Mahmud K, Vance ML. Human growth hormone and aging. New Engl J Med. 2003;348(2):2256–2257.

NAME-YEAR

Mahmud K, Vance ML. 2003. Human growth hormone and aging. New Engl J Med. 348(2):2256–2257.

9. ARTICLE IN A WEEKLY JOURNAL

CITATION-SEQUENCE AND CITATION-NAME

9. Holden C. Future brightening for depression treatments. Science. 2003 Oct 31:810–813.

NAME-YEAR

Holden C. 2003. Future brightening for depression treatments. Science. Oct 31:810–813.

10. ARTICLE IN A MAGAZINE

CITATION-SEQUENCE AND CITATION-NAME

10. Livio M. Moving right along: the accelerating universe holds secrets to dark energy, the Big Bang, and the ultimate beauty of nature. Astronomy. 2002 Jul:34–39.

NAME-YEAR

Livio M. 2002 Jul. Moving right along: the accelerating universe holds secrets to dark energy, the Big Bang, and the ultimate beauty of nature. Astronomy. 34–39.

11. ARTICLE IN A NEWSPAPER

CITATION-SEQUENCE AND CITATION-NAME

11. Kolata G. Bone diagnosis gives new data but no answers. New York Times (National Ed.). 2003 Sep 28;Sect. 1:1 (col. 1).

NAME-YEAR

Kolata G. 2003 Sep 28. Bone diagnosis gives new data but no answers. New York Times (National Ed.). Sect. 1:1 (col. 1).

Electronic Sources

These examples use the citation-sequence or citation-name system. To adapt them to the name-year system, delete the note number and place the update date immediately after the author's name.

The basic entry for most sources accessed through the Internet should include the following elements:

- *Author.* Give the author's name, if available, last name first, followed by the initial(s) and a period.
- *Title.* For book, journal, and article titles, follow the style for print materials. For all other types of electronic material, reproduce the title that appears on the screen.
- *Medium.* Indicate, in brackets, that the source is not in print format by using designations such as [Internet].
- *Place of publication.* The city usually should be followed by the two-letter abbreviation for state. No state abbreviation is necessary for well-known cities such as New York, Chicago, Boston, and London or for a publisher whose location is part of its name (for example, University of Oklahoma Press). If the city is inferred, put the city and

SOURCE MAP: Citing articles from databases using CSE style

Note that date placement will vary depending on whether you are using the citation-sequence or citation-name format or the name-year format.

① *Author.* List all authors' last names first, and use only initials for first and middle names.

②, ⑤ *Publication date.* For name-year format, put publication date after author name(s). For citation-sequence or citation-name format, put it after periodical title. Use year only (for journals) or year month day (for other periodicals).

③ *Title of article.* Capitalize first word and proper nouns/adjectives.

④ *Title of periodical.* Capitalize major words. Abbreviate journal titles. Follow with [*Internet*] and a period.

⑥ *Date of access.* In brackets, write *cited* and year, month, and day. End with a semicolon.

⑦ *Publication information for article.* Give volume number, issue number (in parentheses), a colon, and page numbers. End with a period.

⑧ *Name of database.* End with a period.

⑨ *Publication information for database.* Include the city, the state abbreviation in parentheses, a colon, the publisher's name, and a period.

⑩ *Web address.* Write *Available from* and give the brief URL.

⑪ *Document number.* Write *Document no.* and identifying number.

(Adapted from the CSE guidelines for citing an online journal.)

For an article in a database, use the following formats:

Citation-sequence or citation-name format
1. Last name first initial(s). Title of article. Journal abbreviation [Internet]. Year [cited year month day]; Volume(Issue):Pages. Name of database. City of database publication: Database Publisher. Available from: URL Document No.: number.

Name-year format
Last name first initial(s). Title of article. Journal abbreviation [Internet]. Year [cited year month day]; Volume(Issue):Pages. Name of database. City of database publication: Database Publisher. Available from: URL Document No.: number.

A citation for the article on p. 255 would look like this:

Citation-sequence or citation-name format

NOTE NO. AUTHOR'S LAST NAME, INITIALS   ARTICLE TITLE

1. Miller AL. Epidemiology, etiology, and natural treatment of seasonal affective disorder.

JOURNAL ABBREV.   PUBL. YEAR   DATE OF ACCESS   NAME OF DATABASE

Altern Med Rev [Internet]. 2005 [cited 2006 Aug 9]; 10(1):5-13. Expanded Academic

DATABASE PUBL. CITY   DATABASE PUBL.   PAGE NUMBERS

VOLUME AND ISSUE NUMBER

ASAP. Farmington Hills (MI): Thomson Gale. Available from: http://find.galegroup.com

DOCUMENT NUMBER   URL

Document No.: A131086129.

Name-year format
Miller AL. 2005. Epidemiology, etiology, and natural treatment of seasonal affective disorder. Altern Med Rev [Internet]. [cited 2006 Aug 9]; 10(1):5-13. Expanded Academic ASAP. Farmington Hills (MI): Thomson Gale. Available from: http://find.galegroup.com Document No.: A131086129.

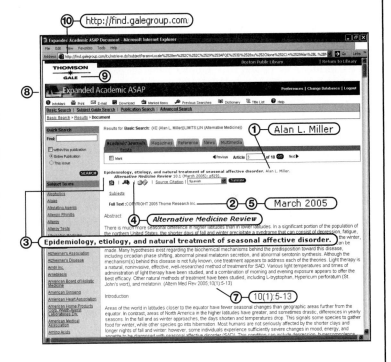

state in brackets. If the city cannot be inferred, use the words *place unknown* in brackets.

- *Publisher.* For Web sites, pages on Web sites, and online databases, include the individual or organization that produces or sponsors the site. If no publisher can be determined, use the words *publisher unknown* in brackets. No publisher is necessary for online journals or journals accessed online.

- *Dates.* Cite three important dates if possible: the date the publication was placed on the Internet or the copyright date; the latest date of any update or revision; and the date the publication was accessed by you.

- *Page, document, volume, and issue numbers.* When citing a portion of a larger work or site, list the inclusive page numbers or document numbers of the specific item being cited. For journals or journal articles, include volume and issue numbers. If exact page numbers are not available, include in brackets the approximate length in computer screens, paragraphs, or bytes: [2 screens], [10 paragraphs], [332K bytes].

- *Address.* Include the URL or other electronic address; use the phrase *Available from:* to introduce the address. Only URLs that end with a slash are followed by a period.

12. MATERIAL FROM AN ONLINE DATABASE

For the basic format for citing an article from a database, see pp. 254–55. (Because CSE does not provide guidelines for citing an article from an online database, this model has been adapted from CSE guidelines for citing an online journal article.)

> 12. Shilts E. Water wanderers. Can Geographic [Internet].
> 2002 [cited 2004 Jan 27]; 122(3):72–77. Expanded Academic
> ASAP. Farmington Hills (MI): Thomson Gale. Available from:
> http://web4.infotrac.galegroup.com/itw/ Document No.:
> A86207443.

13. ARTICLE IN AN ONLINE JOURNAL

13. Perez P, Calonge TM. Yeast protein kinase C. J Biochem [Internet]. 2002 Oct [cited 2003 Nov 3];132(4):513–517. Available from: http://edpex104.bcasj.or.jp/jb-pdf/132-4/jb132-4-513.pdf

14. ARTICLE IN AN ONLINE NEWSPAPER

14. Brody JE. Reasons, and remedies, for morning sickness. New York Times Online [Internet]. 2004 Apr 27 [cited 2004 Apr 30]. Available from: http://www.nytimes.com/2004/04/27/health/27BROD.html

15. ONLINE BOOK

15. Patrick TS, Allison JR, Krakow GA. Protected plants of Georgia [Internet]. Social Circle (GA): Georgia Department of Natural Resources; c1995 [cited 2003 Dec 3]. Available from: http://www.georgiawildlife.com/content/displaycontent.asp?txtDocument=89&txtPage=9

To cite a portion of an online book, give the name of the part after the publication information: *Chapter 6, Encouraging germination*. See model 6.

16. WEB SITE

16. Geology and public policy [Internet]. Boulder (CO): Geological Society of America; c2003 [updated 2003 Apr 8; cited 2003 Apr 13]. Available from: http://www.geosociety.org/science/govpolicy.htm

17. GOVERNMENT WEB SITE

17. Health disparities: minority cancer awareness [Internet]. Atlanta (GA): Centers for Disease Control and Prevention (US); [updated 2004 Apr 27; cited 2005 May 1]. Available from: http://www.cdc .gov/cancer/minorityawareness.htm

A Student Paper, CSE Style

Student Writer

Tara Gupta

The following research proposal by Tara Gupta conforms to the CSE guidelines described in this chapter. Note that these pages have been reproduced in a narrow format to accommodate the book's pocket size.

Field Measurements of
Photosynthesis and Transpiration
Rates in Dwarf Snapdragon
(*Chaenorrhinum minus* Lange):
An Investigation of Water Stress
Adaptations

Tara Gupta

Proposal for a
Summer Research
Fellowship
Colgate University
February 25, 2003

Water Stress Adaptations 2

Introduction

Dwarf snapdragon (*Chaenorrhinum minus*) is a weedy pioneer plant found growing in central New York during spring and summer. Interestingly, the distribution of this species has been limited almost exclusively to the cinder ballast of railroad tracks [1] and to sterile strips of land along highways [2]. In these harsh environments, characterized by intense sunlight and poor soil water retention, one would expect *C. minus* to exhibit anatomical features similar to those of xeromorphic plants (species adapted to arid habitats).

However, this is not the case. T. Gupta and R. Arnold (unpublished) have found that the leaves and stems of *C. minus* are not covered by a thick, waxy cuticle but rather with a thin cuticle that is less effective in inhibiting water loss through diffusion. The root system is not long and thick, capable of reaching deeper, moister soils; instead, it is thin and diffuse, permeating only the topmost (and driest) soil horizon. Moreover, in contrast to many xeromorphic plants, the stomata (pores regulating gas exchange) are not found in sunken crypts or cavities in the epidermis that retard water loss from transpiration.

Water Stress Adaptations 3

Despite a lack of these morphological adaptations to water stress, *C. minus* continues to grow and reproduce when morning dew has been its only source of water for up to 5 weeks (2002 letter from R. Arnold to me). Such growth involves fixation of carbon by photosynthesis and requires that the stomata be open to admit sufficient carbon dioxide. Given the dry, sunny environment, the time required for adequate carbon fixation must also mean a significant loss of water through transpiration as open stomata exchange carbon dioxide with water. How does *C. minus* balance the need for carbon with the need to conserve water?

Purposes of the Proposed Study

The above observations have led me to an exploration of the extent to which *C. minus* is able to photosynthe-size under conditions of low water availability. It is my hypothesis that *C. minus* adapts to these conditions by photosynthesizing in the early morning and late after-noon, when leaf and air temperatures are lower and transpirational water loss is reduced. During the middle of the day, its photosynthetic rate may be very low, perhaps even zero, on hot, sunny afternoons. Similar diurnal changes in photosynthetic rate in response to

Water Stress Adaptations 4

midday water deficits have been described in crop plants [3,4]. There appear to be no comparable studies on non-crop species in their natural habitats.

Thus, the research proposed here aims to help explain the apparent paradox of an organism that thrives in water-stressed conditions despite a lack of morphological adaptations. This summer's work will also serve as a basis for controlled experiments in a plant growth chamber on the individual effects of temperature, light intensity, soil water availability, and other environmental factors on photosynthesis and transpiration rates. These experiments are planned for the coming fall semester.

Methods and Timeline

Simultaneous measurements of photosynthesis and transpiration rates will indicate the balance *C. minus* has achieved in acquiring the energy it needs while retaining the water available to it. These measurements will be taken daily from June 22 to September 7, 2003, at field sites in the Hamilton, NY, area, using an LI-6220 portable photosynthesis system (LICOR, Inc., Lincoln, NE). Basic methodology and use of correction factors will be similar to that described in related studies [5-7]. Data will be collected at regular intervals throughout the

Water Stress Adaptations 5

daylight hours and will be related to measurements of ambient air temperature, leaf temperature, relative humidity, light intensity, wind velocity, and cloud cover.

Budget

1 kg soda lime, 4-8 mesh	$70
(for absorption of CO_2 in photosynthesis analyzer)	
1 kg anhydrous magnesium perchlorate	$130
(used as desiccant for photosynthesis analyzer)	
SigmaScan software (Jandel Scientific Software, Inc.) (for measurement of leaf areas for which photosynthesis and transpiration rates are to be determined)	$195
Estimated 500 miles travel to field sites in own car @ $0.28/mile	$140
CO_2 cylinder, 80 days rental @ $0.25/day	$20
(for calibration of photosynthesis analyzer)	
TOTAL REQUEST	$555

Water Stress Adaptations 6

References

1. Wildrlechner MP. Historical and phenological observations of the spread of *Chaenorrhinum minus* across North America. Can J Bot. 1983;61(1):179–187.

2. Dwarf Snapdragon [Internet]. Olympia (WA): Washington State Noxious Weed Control Board; 2001 [updated 2001 Jul 7; cited 2003 Jan 25]. Available from: http://www.wa.gov/agr/weedboard/weed_info/dwarfsnapdragon.html

3. Boyer JS. Plant productivity and environment. Science. 1982 Nov 6:443–448.

4. Manhas JG, Sukumaran NP. Diurnal changes in net photosynthetic rate in potato in two environments. Potato Res. 1988;31:375–378.

5. Doley DG, Unwin GL, Yates DJ. Spatial and temporal distribution of photosynthesis and transpiration by single leaves in a rainforest tree, *Argyrodendron peralatum*. Aust J Plant Physiol. 1988;15(3):317–326.

6. Kallarackal J, Milburn JA, Baker DA. Water relations of the banana. III. Effects of controlled water stress on water potential, transpiration, photosynthesis and leaf growth. Aust J Plant Physiol. 1990;17(1):79–90.

7. Idso SB, Allen SG, Kimball BA, Choudhury BJ. Problems with porometry: measuring net photosynthesis by leaf chamber techniques. Agron. 1989;81(4):475–479.

8

Research in the Applied Sciences

Resources in the Applied Sciences

GENERAL REFERENCE SOURCES FOR THE APPLIED SCIENCES

Encyclopedia of Physical Science and Technology. 18 vols. 2002. Available in print and online. Consists of over seven hundred entries, each approximately twenty pages in length, on topics such as molecular electronics, image-guided surgery, fiber-optic chemical sensors, self-organizing systems, humanoid robots, pharmacokinetics, and superstring theory.

The International Encyclopedia of Science and Technology. 2000. Includes over sixty-five hundred entries with graphs, photos, and diagrams; a detailed timeline of the development of science since 2500 BC; and a reference section of tables such as SI units, chemical elements, facts about the earth, lists of constellations, and Nobel prize winners.

INDEXES AND DATABASES FOR THE APPLIED SCIENCES

Applied Science and Technology Index. 1958–. Available in print and online. Formerly *Industrial Arts Index*, 1913–1957. Indexes and abstracts nearly four hundred periodicals, concentrating on applied science in areas such as computers, construction, electronics, engineering, the environment, energy sources, geology, technology, telecommunications, and many others. (online)

Government Reports: Annual Index. 1971–. Ceased in print 1990. Indexes and abstracts reports handled through the National Technical Information Service. (online)

Scientific and Technical Information Sources. 1987. Lists resources available in the pure and applied sciences.

WEB RESOURCES FOR THE APPLIED SCIENCES

EurekAlert! Your Global Gateway to Science, Medicine, and Technology News
www.eurekalert.org
> Under the sponsorship of the American Association for the Advancement of Science, posts news of scientific and technological research advances; also includes glossaries, dictionaries, and other reference materials for agriculture, computer sciences, environmental studies, and other fields.

Infomine: Scholarly Internet Resource Collections
lib-www.ucr.edu
> Supplies indexed and annotated links to more than one thousand databases and other resources of academic interest in the physical sciences, including engineering, environmental studies, and computer sciences.

LSU Subject Guides
www.lib.lsu.edu/weblio.html
> Provides extensive annotated guides to Web resources in the applied sciences, including agriculture, computer science, environmental studies, food science, human ecology, and other specialized fields.

New Scientist
www.newscientist.com/weblinks
> Supplies engaging annotated links to selected sites, often on specialized topics, in fields including technology, the Internet, and the environment.

(See also the resources listed for the natural sciences in Chapter 7.)

Agriculture

GENERAL REFERENCE SOURCES FOR AGRICULTURE

Agriculture Handbooks. 1950–. Each volume supplies reliable information on a specific topic.

Encyclopedia of Agricultural Science. 4 vols. 1994. Contains 210 alphabetically arranged articles, each about ten pages in length, covering subjects such as animal science, soil science, agricultural education, biotechnology, pest management, and water resources; includes tables and illustrations. (online)

Yearbook of Agriculture. 1895–1979. Supplies chapters on various aspects of the year's topic.

INDEXES AND DATABASES FOR AGRICULTURE

Agriculture: Illustrated Search Strategy and Sources. 1992. Supplies guidance about using print and electronic reference materials related to agriculture.

Bibliography of Agriculture. 1942–. Ceased in print 2000. Indexes thousands of sources from periodicals, state and federal publications, and reports covering agriculture and related topics. (online)

CRIS/ICAR. 1975–. Supplies information about U.S. and Canadian government-sponsored research on agricultural topics.

WEB RESOURCES FOR AGRICULTURE

Agricultural Research Service: U.S. Department of Agriculture
www.ars.usda.gov
Supplies news and research information as well as links to major agriculture databases and resources, including the National Agricultural Library.

CRIS: Current Research Information Service
cris.csrees.usda.gov
Under the auspices of the U.S. Department of Agriculture, reports on thousands of current federal and state research projects on agriculture, forestry, food, and nutrition.

CSU Bioweb: California State University Biological Sciences Web Server
arnica.csustan.edu
> Links to many resources on specialized biological fields such as agriculture, including government resources, multimedia information, and other useful servers and sites.

National Agricultural Library
www.nal.usda.gov
> Provides its own collection of materials and images on agriculture, and consolidates access to resources through AgNIC (Agriculture Network Information Center) and other Web sites on animal science, economics, food science, forestry, natural resources, nutrition, range land, and other agriculture-related topics.

(See also the resources listed for the life sciences in Chapter 7 on the natural sciences.)

Computer Science

GENERAL REFERENCE SOURCES FOR COMPUTER SCIENCE

Dictionary of Computer Science, Engineering, and Technology. 2001. Provides detailed definitions for over eight thousand terms that cover topics such as telecommunication, information theory, artificial intelligence, programming language, privacy issues, and software and hardware systems.

Dictionary of Computing. 2004. Defines over ten thousand terms, concepts, and technologies from various areas of computing, such as software, hardware, networking, mainframes, the Internet, multimedia, and programming. (online)

McGraw-Hill Encyclopedia of Electronics and Computers. 1988. Includes heavily illustrated articles on the design, materials, functioning, and uses of electronic devices.

Oryx Sourcebook Series in Computer and Information Science. 1988. Supplies concise discussions of major topics related to computer programs and software, networks, systems, and computation.

Prentice-Hall Encyclopedia of Information Technology. 1987. Supplies articles
on a wide range of topics, including languages, components (such
as monitors), and applications (such as bar codes and telephone networks).

**INDEXES AND DATABASES FOR
COMPUTER SCIENCE**

ACM Guide to Computing Literature. 1977–1997. Formerly *ACM Bibliography
and Subject Index,* 1963–1976. Indexes articles about data, computation, hardware, software, systems, applications, and other computer-
related topics. (online)

WEB RESOURCES FOR COMPUTER SCIENCE

The Collection of Computer Science Bibliographies
liinwww.ira.uka.de/bibliography/index.html
Provides access to over one thousand bibliographies on computer
technology, programming, and research, with references to articles,
reports, and presentations arranged by subject area.

Developer.com
www.developer.com
Supplies career information, free graphics, and access to thousands
of resources on computer technology and topics such as servers,
databases, and Web sites, all oriented to professional computer
developers.

PC Webopedia
www.pcwebopedia.com
Provides keyword and topical searches on a vast range of terms and
topics related to personal computers and computing technology.

The WWW Virtual Library — Computing and Computer Science
www.vlib.org/Computing
Includes access to bibliographies, indexes, and a dictionary of computer terminology, as well as resources in specialty areas as diverse
as artificial intelligence, telecommunications, computational linguistics, and cryptography.

Engineering

GENERAL REFERENCE SOURCES FOR ENGINEERING

Annual Book of ASTM Standards. 1970–. Supplies many volumes, published annually, that detail the specifications, practices, and other guidelines necessary to meet the standards of the American Society for Testing and Materials (ASTM) for products as diverse as plastics, paint, soap, metals and alloys, textiles, and paper.

ASTM Dictionary of Engineering, Science and Technology. 2005. Supplies concise definitions derived from technical committee–developed standards for ASTM terminology.

CRC Handbook of Tables for Applied Engineering Science. 1970–; biennial. Provides basic tables and data for the various engineering fields.

Encyclopedia of Materials Science and Engineering. 8 vols. 1986-1993. Supplies entries on the nature and use of fibers, plastics, and other materials.

Handbook of Engineering Fundamentals. 1990. Provides essential information for the varied fields of engineering, including equations, laws, theorems, properties, and statistical data. (online)

Handbook of Industrial Engineering. 2001. Includes formulas and data for industrial engineering.

IEEE 100: The Authoritative Dictionary of IEEE Standards Terms. 2000. Supplies authoritative explanations of terms and standards approved by the Institute of Electrical and Electronics Engineers (IEEE).

The Illustrated Dictionary of Electronics. 2001. Provides over 27,500 definitions, many with illustrations, of terms in fields that include computers, robotics, lasers, television, radio, and IC technology.

Marks' Standard Handbook for Mechanical Engineers. 1978–. Provides essential information for mechanical engineering, including mathematical data, technical standards, and environmental issues. (online)

McGraw-Hill Concise Encyclopedia of Engineering. 2005. Supplies articles on major topics in the many fields of engineering. (online)

Perry's Chemical Engineer's Handbook. 1997. Includes essential specific information for the chemical engineer. (online)

Standard Handbook for Civil Engineers. 2004. Supplies fundamental information for civil engineers, including specifications, construction, design, and management. (online)

Standard Handbook for Electrical Engineers. 2000. Includes necessary reference material for the electrical engineer on topics related to the production, use, and conversion of electrical power.

Standard Handbook of Environmental Engineering. 1999. Supplies essential information about air and water quality, water management, waste disposal, and related topics. (online)

INDEXES AND DATABASES FOR ENGINEERING

Engineering Index Monthly. 1884–. Formerly *Engineering Index.* Indexes and abstracts periodical articles, books, patents, and some conference papers on engineering. (online)

INSPEC. 1969–. A database containing citations to journals, conference proceedings, books, reports, and dissertations in physics, electrical engineering and electronics, computers, and information technology. (online)

WEB RESOURCES FOR ENGINEERING

ASCE's Civil Engineering Database
www.pubs.asce.org/cedbsrch.html
 Provides access to over eighty thousand bibliographic and abstracted records in civil engineering since 1975.

EEVL: The Internet Guide to Engineering, Mathematics, and Computing
www.eevl.ac.uk/index.htm
 Provides access to quality networked engineering, mathematics, and computing resources for students, staff, and researchers in higher education.

Electronic Engineers' Toolbox
www.eg3.com/ebox.htm
 A search utility for specialized issues within electronics engineering. Provides links to both commercial and noncommercial resources.

IEEE Spectrum
www.spectrum.ieee.org

Provides access to all major publications and resources of the Institute of Electrical and Electronics Engineers.

Institute of Electrical and Electronics Engineers
www.ieee.org
> Links to member services, related technical societies, search engines, databases, publications, and activities.

Mechanical Design Engineering Resources
www.gearhob.com
> Lists everything from industry associations to research and development sites.

The WWW Virtual Library — Chemical Engineering
www.che.ufl.edu/www-che
> Offers a specific subtopic list and links to meetings, conferences, organizations, and information resources.

The WWW Virtual Library — Civil Engineering
www.ce.gatech.edu/WWW-CE/home.html
> Lists servers containing information on civil engineering, most of them from university programs.

The WWW Virtual Library — Electrical and Electronics Engineering
www.cem.itesm.mx/vlib
> A good place to start.

The WWW Virtual Library — Engineering
www.vlib.org/Enginnering
> Lists links to many relevant sources across engineering fields, including all the engineering virtual libraries, from acoustic engineering to welding engineering. Includes information on standards, products, and institutions.

Environmental Studies

GENERAL REFERENCE SOURCES FOR ENVIRONMENTAL STUDIES

A Dictionary of Ecology, Evolution, and Systematics. 1998. Defines over eleven thousand concepts, methodologies, and strategies in disciplines such as botany, zoology, bacteriology, mineralogy, and paleontology.

Dictionary of Energy. 2006. Supplies entries with illustrations defining energy-related terms and drawing on scientific, technological, engineering, and economics viewpoints.

Encyclopedia of Environmental Science. 2000. Includes over 340 entries on subjects ranging from alkalinity, dams and reservoirs, and ecological modeling in forestry to renewable resources, urban ecology, and volcanoes.

Encyclopedia of Environmental Science and Technology. 2 vols. 2000. Supplies extensive articles on many aspects of this field, ranging from environmental law and urban planning to hydrology, microbiology, and sulfur removal.

Encyclopedia of Water. 2003. Covers water-related topics such as use, quality, management, and legislation; includes maps, illustrations, and statistical data.

Facts on File Dictionary of Environmental Science. 2001. Includes brief entries on key terms in environmental studies and related fields, such as engineering, law, and computer modeling.

Grzimek's Encyclopedia of Ecology. 1976–. Supplies chapters and maps on such topics as habitats, environmental factors, pollutants, and other influences on the environments of both animals and humans.

McGraw-Hill Encyclopedia of Environmental Science and Engineering. 1993. Provides introductory essays and extensive alphabetical entries on major topics in environmental studies; includes references and illustrations.

United States Energy Atlas. 1986. Supplies explanatory text, figures, and other illustrations with maps to analyze and locate available energy resources.

INDEXES AND DATABASES FOR ENVIRONMENTAL STUDIES

Ecological Abstracts. 1980–. Indexes and abstracts articles from over two thousand periodicals and books. (online)

Environment Abstracts. 1971–. Supplies abstracts of articles from over five thousand periodicals on topics such as natural resources, pollution, energy, ecology, wildlife, and related areas. (online)

Environmental Periodicals Bibliography. 1972–. Lists the contents of hundreds of periodicals, including popular publications, on environmental topics such as natural resources, ecology, air quality, and energy. (online)

Pollution Abstracts. 1970–. Supplies abstracts of articles from journals and nontechnical publications about air, water, and other types of pollution, as well as waste management, sewage treatment, radiation, noise control, and related topics. (online)

WEB RESOURCES FOR ENVIRONMENTAL STUDIES

CIESIN: Information for a Changing World
www.ciesin.org

Provides scientific data, interactive services, guides to major environmental topics, and access to other resources on the global environment and environmental resources, all under the auspices of the Consortium for International Earth Science Information Network.

EnviroInfo: Environmental Information Sources
www.deb.uminho.pt/fontes/enviroinfo

Provides links to many resources useful for environmental studies of air, water, soil, pollution, waste, ecology, legal issues, and other topics.

EnviroLink
www.envirolink.org

Supplies interactive services, news, and educational and activist information, as well as many links to environmental resources, broadly defined and grouped by category.

National Geophysical Data Center
www.ngdc.noaa.gov

Consolidates information—including satellite data—for environmental and related studies.

U.S. Environmental Protection Agency (EPA)
www.epa.gov

Organizes environmental information for various types of users (including citizens, students, and researchers) and by topic (such as news, projects, and publications), including other resources, clear-inghouses, and databases.

AIP Style

Writers in the sciences and applied sciences, including those in the fields of physics, applied physics, optics, astrophysics, and acoustics, use the documentation and format style of the American Institute of Physics. Guidelines for citing print and electronic sources may be found in the *AIP Style Manual,* Fourth Edition (1990).

Many journals and fields in the applied sciences use modifications of AIP style or their own preferred methods for documenting sources and formatting papers. The various branches of engineering, for instance, have different requirements for citations. If your instructor does not specify a style, be sure to ask which one is preferred in that field.

DIRECTORY TO AIP STYLE

In-Text Notes

List of Notes

BOOKS

1. Book by one author, *277*
2. Book by two or three authors, *278*
3. Book by more than three authors, *278*
4. Book by a corporate or group author, *278*
5. Several sections cited from one edited book in one note, *278*

PERIODICALS

6. Article in a journal paginated by volume, *279*
7. Article in a journal paginated by issue, *279*

(Continued)

AIP Format for In-Text Notes

The AIP recommends using in-text notes—superscript numbers in the text, numbered consecutively—to mark citations of sources. The references to which the superscript numbers refer are then presented in a double-spaced list of notes at the end of the paper, following the same numerical order. A single number and note may refer to several sources as long as all of them are relevant to the point in the text.

The preliminary work by Grever[1] and Martino[2] defined the essential experimental variables. Later studies by Throckworth et al.[3] and Wixell[4] have confirmed the validity of this approach.

AIP Format for a List of Notes

Books

1. BOOK BY ONE AUTHOR

Supply the author's name, first name first. Use initials only or spell out a name in full, just as it appears on the title page.

[1] J. A. Poppiti, Practical Techniques for Laboratory Analysis (Lewis, Boca Raton, FL, 1994), p. 35.

2. BOOK BY TWO OR THREE AUTHORS

[2] M. Born and E. Wolf, Principles of Optics, 6th ed. (Pergamon, Oxford, 1980), p. 143.

3. BOOK BY MORE THAN THREE AUTHORS

Use *et al.* freely in the text of your paper, but avoid it in the list of notes unless there are three or more authors.

[3] Lillian Hoddeson et al., Critical Assembly: A Technical History of Los Alamos During the Oppenheimer Years, 1943–45 (Cambridge University Press, New York, 1993).

4. BOOK BY A CORPORATE OR GROUP AUTHOR

[4] American National Standards Institute, American National Standard for Human Factors Engineering of Visual Display Terminal Workstations, ANSI/HFS 100-1988 (Human Factors Society, Santa Monica, CA, 1988).

5. SEVERAL SECTIONS CITED FROM ONE EDITED BOOK IN ONE NOTE

[5] John J. Sarraille and Thomas A. Gentry, in Computer-Mediated Communication and the Online Classroom, edited by Zane L. Berge and Mauri P. Collins (Hampton Press, Cresskill, NJ, 1995), Chap. 9, pp. 137–150; Raleigh C. Muns, ibid., Chap. 10, pp. 151–164.

Periodicals

6. ARTICLE IN A JOURNAL PAGINATED BY VOLUME

[6] S. J. Lee, K. Imen, and S. D. Allen, J. Appl. Phys. **74**, 7046 (1993).

7. ARTICLE IN A JOURNAL PAGINATED BY ISSUE

Check with your instructor about whether you should include page numbers for an entire article or a specific page reference.

[7] John Reason, Elec. World **207** (7), 33–42 (1993).

8. ARTICLE CITATION INCLUDING TITLE

Check with your instructor about whether you should or should not include article titles.

[8] S. J. Lee, K. Imen, and S. D. Allen, "Shock wave analysis or laser assisted particle removal," J. Appl. Phys. **74**, 7046 (1993).

9. SEVERAL ARTICLES BY THE SAME AUTHOR(S) IN THE SAME JOURNAL

[9] Zhiqiang Wu and P. Paul Ruber, J. Appl. Phys. **74**, 6240 (1993); **71**, 1318 (1992).

10. SEVERAL ARTICLES BY THE SAME AUTHOR(S) IN DIFFERENT JOURNALS

[10] S. M. Gates, J. Phys. Chem. **96**, 10439–10443 (1992); Surface Sci. **195**, 307 (1988).

11. SEVERAL ARTICLES BY DIFFERENT AUTHOR(S) IN THE SAME JOURNAL

Use *ibid.* to show that the articles are "in the same place."

[11] A. C. Kibblewhite and C. Y. Wu, J. Acoust. Soc. Am. **94**, 36 (1993); G. Haralabus et al., ibid. **94**, 3385 (1993).

Electronic Sources

12. COMPUTER PROGRAM

If the author's name is known, add it to the citation.

[12] SuperCalc3 Release 2.1 (Computer Associates, Micro Products Division, San Jose, CA, 1985).

13. INTERNET SOURCE

The *AIP Style Manual* does not provide guidelines for citing source material from the Internet, and different journals published by the AIP follow different guidelines for such sources. Here are examples of citations that have appeared in such journals.

[13] M. Steyvers and J. B. Tenenbaum, 2001, preprint, www-psych.stanford.edu/~jbt/.

[13] P. Baran, Introduction to Distributed Communications Networks, RM-3420-PR, August 1964, http://www.rand.org/publications/RM/baran.list.html.

Other Sources

14. PERSONAL COMMUNICATION

[14] J. Kincaid (private communication).